Luís de Camões, Richard Francis

**The lyricks**

sonnets, canzons, odes, and sextines

Luís de Camões, Richard Francis

**The lyricks**
*sonnets, canzons, odes, and sextines*

ISBN/EAN: 9783744789004

Printed in Europe, USA, Canada, Australia, Japan

Cover: Foto ©Thomas Meinert / pixelio.de

More available books at **www.hansebooks.com**

(*SONNETS, CANZONS, ODES, AND SEXTINES*)

*ENGLISHED BY*

# RICHARD F. BURTON,

*And imprinted for the Translator at London in October,* 1884.

———

LONDON :

BERNARD QUARITCH,

15 PICCADILLY.

1884.

"Wherefore I bisekke you mekely that ye praye for me that God foryeve me my giltes, and nameliche of my translaciouns."

*Parsones Tale* (by *Le grand translateur*).

"The things given to the public as poems of Camoens are no more to be found in the original Portuguese than they are in the Song of Solomon."

BYRON.

De pocos ha de ser mi voz oida;
Passen los años, y serà estimada.

LOPE DE VEGA.

فتقل للشامتين بنا رويدا
اعاجكم المصايب و الخطرات

Intendami chi può, che m' intendo io.

*Ital. Prov.*

TO

THE PRINCE OF THE LYRIC POETS OF HIS DAY,

# ALGERNON CHARLES SWINBURNE.

———◦———

MY DEAR SWINBURNE,

Accept the unequal exchange, my brass for your gold.  Your "Poems and Ballads" began to teach the Philister what might there is in the music of language, and what the marvel of lyric inspiration, far subtler and more æthereal than mere poetry, means to the mind of man.

Without more ado, allow me to excuse this "transaction" by a something which comes from the East :—

"A poor man, passing by one day when his King travelled, brought him a little water with both hands, saying :—'Drink, my lord, for the heat is great.' He accepted it gladly from him, not looking to the small quality of that service, but only to the good-will with which it was offered."

Believe me ever,

Your old friend and fellow-traveller,

RICHARD F. BURTON.

DESTERRO, TRIESTE,
*Sept.* 25, 1884.

# THE TRANSLATOR'S FOREWORD.

I now submit to the Public a second section of my Master's works, the first Part of his far-famed Lyricks. This volume is the fifth of a Camonian series; and two or three more, which are in MS., will complete my Labour of Love.

It is hard to repress a smile at the thought of these pages being turned over by Young England of the nineteenth century;—these Sonnets which date from days when "courting" was a study; these Odes that deal with old Endymion and Achilles, whose second death was after the date of Gray; these Canzons so full of shadowy half-expression, of shorthand allusiveness, that every Commentator explains them for himself. To the inevitable *cui bono?* I can only plead a "call": my translation should be printed even though it had ne'er a reader save the writer. It is innocuous so far that it can injure no publisher: it is brought out *sumptu meo;* and my friend Mr. Quaritch is strong enough to lend his name without fearing to lose caste. And yet, though my work must be its own reward, I am not wholly without hope that the

healthy, manly, hearty old song will find its little
meed of appreciation if not of praise.

In this volume I follow the lines laid down for myself
in "The Lusiads"; especially the use of archaicisms
and of eclectic style. Both still appear to me neces-
sary when translating a poet older than Shakespeare.
Over-polish has been especially avoided: the *labor
limæ* of the classics, and the "filing and finishing"
of our older writers, was everywhere applied by my
Poet to his Epos, not always to his minor pieces.
This copy is naught if not perfectly faithful to its
original; showing Camoens to the English reader in
English dress. At the same time, I have borne in
mind Rosetti's dictum—"the life-blood of rhythmical
translation is, that a good poem should not be turned
into a bad one."

Again: despite Denham's denunciation of literal-
ism,—

> That servile path thou nobly dost decline
> Of tracing word by word and line by line;

despite Johnson, who quotes with approval,—

> These are the labour'd birth of slavish brain,
> Not the effect of poetry but pain;

and despite the superficial popular paradox, "A literal
translation is no translation at all," I have done my
best to translate *verbatim et literatim;* not though by
thought, but word by word. Goethe finally laid down
the law thus:—"There are two maxims of Translation. The one requires that the author of a foreign

nation be brought to us in such manner that we regard him as our own; the other, on the contrary,
demands that we transport ourselves to him, and
adopt his situation, his mode of speaking, his pecu-
liarities." For authority may be quoted the great
example of my Master, who, in his *Triumphos*,
translated from Petrarch's *Trionfi*, sinks his indi-
viduality and attempts the replica. Here once more
I have aimed at " Englishing " the style, the idioms,
the *ipsissima verba* of Camoens; I have attempted
not only fidelity, but literality, by making the most
conscientious possible portrait. Perfection may be
unattainable in this matter; but the more we strive
for the *beau idéal* of translation the less we waste our
time and our trouble.

A few words concerning the contents of this volume.
By way of general preface I have prefixed the original
Prologo of Camoens' Lyricks which ushered in the
Editio Princeps of the Rhythmas. The Poems follow in
the order adopted by their earliest Portuguese editors,
Faria y Sousa; Joseph Lopes Ferreira; Visconde
de Juromenha, and the Bibliotheca da Actualidade
(Theophilo Braga). For facility of reference the
initial lines of the texts have been prefixed to the
translations. In Appendix I. I have offered a few
observations upon the Lyricks of the "Portuguese
Apollo." To avoid troubling my readers and cum-
bering my pages with notes I have inserted the few
absolutely required into the Index of First Lines
(Appendix II.), after the fashion of certain Portuguese

editions. Most of the subjects treated in the Rhythmas have already been noticed in "Camoens, his Life and his Lusiads"; and to these two volumes the student is referred.

It may conciliate some enmities and captivate, perhaps, some good-will when I abjure all pretensions to rank as a Poet. No one more fully appreciates the difference between "making" and translating; between the Poétes (the Creator) and the copier who aspires only to second prizes, to "increase the returns or revenues of knowledge, but not the stock or inheritance." My ambition is limited to the humbler boast,—

> Pus dieus m' a dat saber
> E entendemen ver
> De trobar, etc.

Also let me request English readers, who would form a critical estimate of the Camonian Sonnet, to renew their acquaintance with those of Shakespeare and Spenser. Finally they might oblige me by remembering the weighty words of Milton :—"Books are not dead things, but do contain, as in a phiall, the potent efficacy of the spirit that bred them." They will not find a nobler spirit than Camoens.

In preparing this volume I have been aided by a host of "with-workers." Amongst them I must mention with cordial expressions of gratitude the names of my correspondents, M. J. J. Aubertin and Dr. Wilhelm Storck, Professor der deutschen Sprache und Literatur, at Münster. This learned German,

the first translator of all Camoens' Obras, has not
only published in five volumes the Redondilhas and
Letters (1); the Sonnets (2); the Elegies, Sextines,
Odes and Octaves (3); the Canzons and Idylls,
or Eclogues (4); The Lusiads (5); and the Theatre
(6); he has, moreover, illustrated his versions with
critical notes and text-emendations which are most
valuable to the student of Camoens.

RICHARD F. BURTON.

# PROLOGO

## FERNANDO RODRIGUES LOBO SURRUPITA.

*(Editor's Preface to his Readers.)*

———◦◦———

WHEREAS this Book must come into the hands of the many; and whereas it were impossible that all should be equal in the knowledge of things required for its intendiment, meseemeth not a little profitable to advert briefly upon some of the subjects; such, for instance, as the title and the distribution of the work, and also the author thereof. And, beginning with the title, the term *Rhythmas* (which the Italians and the French pronounce without the aspirates) descendeth from 'Ρυθμὸς, a Greek vocable signifying *Number* or *Harmony*. Thus declare *Diomedes Grammaticus* and *Nicoláo Perotto*,[1] in the "Cornucopia," the Commentary on the fourth Epigram. In either signification it applieth especially to the verse of Italian measure; because this consisteth not only of a certain number of syllables, but also containeth the Harmony produced by the Accents and the Consonants (rhymes); as proveth *Benedetto Varchi*[2] in his *Dialogo Tusculano* (Enquiry IX.). Nor doth this admit of doubt, for the Corpus of every manner of Poem is composed of *Number* and *Harmony*, whence the definition of *Posidonius*, the *Stoick*,—"Numbered Diction," consisting of a certain measure or metre, as *Laertius* hath it in his Life of *Zeno*. So true it is that Socrates, having been counselled by an Oracle that, if he would attain to happiness, he must apply his mind to Musick, understood thereby that he would satisfy the intent of such counsel by employing himself wholly in making Verses, the Numbers or Harmony of which are part of the same Musick, even as relateth *Celio Calcagnino*,[3] in the Oration which he made in Praise of the Arts. Hence also proceeded the Etymology of this term "Poet," which, conformably with the opinion of Eustathius, followed by *Rhodiginus*[4] in his fourth Book, is derived from ποιεῖν in the sense of ἐμμέτρως ἀείδειν, meaning *cantare*, to sing. This wise also affirmeth the same *Nicolão Perotto* (on the fifth Epigram); and, therefore, Dante called Poetry[5] a "rhetorical Fiction set to Musick."

That the Title of *Rhythmas* besitteth this work also appeareth clearly from a Discourse made by Cardinal Pietro Bembo,[6] in the second Book of his *Prosas*, wherein he saith that *Rhythmas* (or "*Rimas*," as he writeth the word) be of three modes; for they are either *regulate* or they are *free*, or they are partly *free* and partly *regulate*.

*Regulate* we term those *Rhythmas* which are ever

subject to one and the same Rule; such be the
"Tercets," or triple rhymes, of which *Dante* is supposed to have been the inventor, for that, before
him, they were made by none.[7] Regulate also are the
"Octaves" (*Ottava rima*) devised by the *Sicilians*,
who assigned to each of them only two Consonants
or Rhymes: the same were afterwards reduced to
a better form by the *Tuscans*, a third Consonant in
the last Couplet being introduced by them. Of this
sort, further, were the "Sextines," an invention of
the *Provençaux*, especially of *Arnaldo Daniel*.[8]

Free Rhythmas are those which do not keep any
Rule, either in the Number of the Verses or in the
Correspondence of the Consonants. Such is the
"Madrigal,"[9] derived from *Mandra*, a Tuscan vocable,
this being a Composition of *Villeins*, or country-folk,
and corresponding with our Portingall *Villancetes*.

Rhythmas partly *free* and partly *regulate* be those
which in some things go subject to Rule, and which
in others are exempted from it. Of such sort are
the "Sonnet" and the "Canzon"; for Sonnets, although obliged to follow the same Rule in the Number and in the Disposition of their Verses, withal, in
the Correspondence of Consonants, they have no
certain obligeance. This was shown by *Rengifo*[10] in
his *Ars Poetica* (Cap. XLIII.), wherein, however, he
followeth the Observations made with abundant Judge-
ment and Genius by *Torquato Tasso* in his *Dialogo
della Poesia Toscana*. The "Canzons"[11] partake of
the same Nature, as is pointed out by the same

*Rengifo* (Cap. LIX. *et seq.*).    Saying thus much we
have justified the Title.

Followeth the *Distribution* of the work, which
is divided into five parts, because the Number
quinary especially appertaineth to works of Poesy
and of Eloquence.    This is clearly seen for-that
conformably with the doctrine of the *Platonists*, it
was dedicated to *Mercurius* and to other gods, who,
according to their gentilick rite, were the *Patrons* of
the *Arts*, as Rhodiginus writeth (Lib. xii. Cap. 10),
and they held *Mercurius* to be the *Deity* of *Eloquence ;*
and therefore, as relat·th *Vincencio Cartario*,[12] in his
Book on the " Images of the Gods," they consecrated
to him the *Tongues* (of victims).    This being the case
with *Eloquence*, the same became that of *Poetry*, by
virtue of the alliance subsisting between the twain ;
agreeably to the definition of *Dante* and *Posidonius*.
And therefore the fifth letter of the *Greek* alphabet
was dedicated to *Apollo*, as writeth *Guillelmus
Onciacus*,[13] in his " Book of Places " (*Numeralium
Locorum Decas*, Cap. V.).    Also of the *Muses*, albeit
they number *nine*, only *five* had the Government of
Poesy ; because to *Clio* was attributed the *Subject* of
Verse, she presiding over History ; to *Polymnia* the
adornment of Language ; the Epos Heroical to
*Calliope ;* to *Melpomene* the Tragick ; and to *Thalia*
the Comick, conformably with the vulgar *Epigram*
which goeth amongst those of Virgilius.

Following, then, such *Distribution*, we have assigned
the First Place to the *Sonnets*, these being Compo-

sitions of the highest *Merit* by reason of their Difficulty; for not only do they refuse admittance either to an idle *word* or to a word of little *weight*, they must also include the whole of their Subject-matter within the term of fourteen Lines; and they must be closed by the last *Tercet* in such sort that the understanding feel no desire to pass onwards, a matter wherein many *Poets* who fly upon the wings of *Fame* have not proved themselves happy.[14]

The second place was given to the *Odes* which correspond with *Verses Lyrical*, as showeth Fernando de Herrera [15] in his most erudite "Commentary" on the first *Canzon* of *Garcilasso*. The third to the *Elegies* and to the *Octaves*, forms which we cannot find that Petrarch used,[16] whilst both were cultivated with great felicity by *Ariosto;* and, peradventure, he knew better to imitate, in the perfection of Elegiack Verse, *Tibullus* and *Propertius* (who be the Princes of this Genus) than *Virgilius* in the Majesty of the Heroick. Fourthly come the *Eclogues* because 'tis a species of composition which requireth less competency; and in this form, leaving aside *Theocritus* and *Virgilius*, especial excellence was attained by *Sannazaro,* as also by *Bernardino Rota* in his *Piscatory Eclogues.*[17] The fifth and final place was assigned to the *Grosas,* the *Voltas* and other compositions in short (octosyllabic) verse, which are peculiar to our Spain.[18] In these *Gregorio Sylvestre* [19] showed notable superiority amongst all the *Spaniards;* of a truth he would have held the first place had it not been taken from him by LUIS DE CAMOENS for the acuteness of his conceits and the propriety of his Diction, as well as for the ability of submitting to impossible Rules, an ability which he displayed much more in his other *Rhythmas*, as we shall presently say.

And pursuing with the *Poet* (which be the third part of this Prologue), it were evident *Rashness* to attempt his Eulogy. For albeit many others won *Fame* in some individual *Perfection;* natheless not a few of them wanted the natural Disposition which would have made easy to them the contexture of *Verse;* hence they elaborated it with such Asperity and Difficulty that they would seem to deflower their words and to beget upon them Conceits par force,[20] and thus they fail of this *Suavity* wherein *Poesy* herself consists, agreeably to the Doctrine of *Fracastorius* in his "Dialogue" entitled *Naugerio* and taken from *Horatius* and *Quintilianus.* Others again, who drew nearer to Nature, fell short either because they were unhappy in choice of *Terms;* or because they lacked the *Wealth* of *Words* wherewith to attire and to adorn Speech, together with the *Beauties* of Language, such as the Tropes and Figures, without which *Cicero* and *Virgilius* never spake; or, finally, because they employ expressions so homely and commonplace, as if the very constitution of *Poesy* were not Elevation above vulgar usage, conformably with the opinion of *Plutarchus* in his Tractate, "De Poesiis" and of Rhodiginus (Lib. iv. Cap. 4). Others, who have better Gifts of *Language* possess no *Learning* wherewith to illustrate their works; it being a Truth (as saith Rhodiginus in Cap. 2 of the same Book), that they only may be lawfully entitled *Poets* who displayed a knowledge of various Sciences, as did *Orpheus, Homeros, Virgilius* and *Pindaros*.

Now, LUIS DE CAMOENS, on the other hand, is so far removed from all such Defects that we see in him conjointly the promptest natural *Disposition* to express his Thoughts, accompanied with an innate *Facility* which fills his Verse with Sweetness; and, withal, a Diction so pure, so ornate with all the Splendours of *Eloquence*, and so rich in the *Conceits* and *Jewels* of every *Science*, that it would seem as if in him alone Art and Nature had conjoined every requisite for rising to the height of Poesy.

And besides being excellent in all modes of Rhythmas, especially in shorter Verse, as we have already said, he is most happy in the Canzon,[21] keeping every Law of that Composition in such manner that he hath no cause to envy *Petrarch, Bembo,* and *Garcilasso,* who are the most lauded in this department. And he holdeth the same Place in the greater part of his Sonnets; and he would have held it all had not some, which do here figure as his, been thrown off with scanty care at the importunity of *Friends*. Hence it happens that oft-times they came to aid those who asked aid, with more of haste than of the obligatory *filing* and *finishing;* and, finally, they are printed as his without the will of the Author.

This is not the Place to treat of the Style heroical:

the task may be left to him who shall comment upon The *Lusiada*.[22]   But what may here be said is that our Poet carried out so literally and so completely the Obligations of the *Epos*, that if it did not seem *Arrogance* we might assign to him a Seat hard by that occupied by *Virgilius ;* for in the Grandeur, the Gravity, and the Harmony of the *Words ;* in the Tracing and the Discursus of the *Work*, and in the Sublimity of the *Subject*, he everywhere followed *Virgilius* his footsteps.   And in all his *Fictions* and *Allegories*, without which there can be no Heroick Poem (agreeably to the opinion of Aristotle as quoted by Rhodiginus in the same Lib. iv. Cap. 4 ; and to the writings of *Plutarchus*, who in the place above referred to reprehends *Empedocles*, *Parmenides*, *Nicandros* and *Theognides* for usurping the name of *Poet*, because they wrote verses rich only in Learning but unaccompanied by Imagination), in this matter, I say, he showed a genius so admirable as well nigh to rival *Homeros*.   Would that he had been able to abase his Grandeur in some of his Eclogues by conforming them more with the style *Bucolick*.[23]

And although our Poet lack not *Detractors* to calumniate his *Works*, yet doth Detraction by no means obscure their *Desarts*.   For both *Virgilius* and *Homeros* underwent this trial, which naturally awaits all rare and seld-seen Genius.   So true it is that the *Grammarian Carvilius*[24] writ a whole book upon the Errors of *Virgilius :* also *Caligula*, the *Cæsar*, dared affirm that the Poet had neither Ability nor Erudi-

tion; and resolved upon sending an Order to burn
all his *Works* and *Portraits* stored in sundry Biblio-
thecæ. So relate *Suetonius Tranquillus* and *Pedro
Crinito* in " De Poetis Latinis," libri iii.[25]

And now remaineth only to remind the *Reader*
that the *Errors* met with in this Impression were
neither neglected nor unobserved by him who assisted
in copying the Book.[26] But it was deemed a lesser
inconvenience to let them appear as they were found
(collating them, however, with certain *Hand-books*
wherein the *Works* were quoted fragmentarily), than
to violate the *Compositions* of another, without an
evident Certainty that the *Emendations* would be true
and correct. For all good understandings will re-
serve the Right of Judgment that these be not
*Errors* of the *Author*, but the Cankers of *Time* and
the careless Inadvertency of *Copyists*. And here we
follow what approved itself to *Augustus Cæsar* who,
in the Commission entrusted by him to *Varius* and
to *Tucca*, expressly forbade them to change anything
of *Virgilius* or to add aught of their own. For this
would be, in fine, to confound the *Substance* of the
Verses and the Author's *Conceits* with the Emenda-
tor's *Words* and *Inventions* without consequent assurance, withal, of the readings being either original or
emended. Here, therefore, no action has been taken
save only in whatsoever clearly shows itself to be a
*Fault* of the *Pen :* the remainder goes forth even as it
was found written, and very different from what it
would have been had LUIS DE CAMOENS printed it

during his Life-term. But even thus, and despite the Injuries of Time and Ignorance, the *Light* of our Poet's *Merits* shines with splendour sufficient to prevent our envying in this *Form* of *Poesy* any stranger *People*.

(Signed)   FERNÃO RODRIGUES LOPO SURRUPITA,
*Licentiate and Advocate in this Court.*[7]

# NOTES.

THE following remarks upon the "Prologo" are borrowed from various sources. And here I take with pleasure the opportunity of acknowledging the able and friendly assistance of my learned friend, the Petrarchist, Dr. Attilio Hortis, chief librarian to the *Museo Civico*, Trieste.

[1] Diomedes Grammaticus (before 6th century) wrote : " De Oratione et Partibus Orationis, et vario Genere Metrorum Libri III." ad Athanasium (Hephæstion edit. Gaisford, pp. 431–42). Nicolão Perotto (Nicolaus Perottus), born in 1430 at Sassoferrato ; professed Poetry and Rhetoric at Bologna 1452) ; was raised by Pius II. to the Archbishopric and Governorship of Umbria, Spoleto, and Perugia, and died in 1480. Amongst many works famous in his day, he left one " De Metris, sive de Genere Metrorum;" Venet. 1497. For further details see Part III., Sect. 1, p. 695, "Lehrbuch einer Literaturgeschichte," by Dr. Johann G. Th. Grasse ; Dresden and Leipzig, 1837.

[2] The well-known Benedetto Varchi, of Florence (born on March 19, 1503 ; died about æt. 62), of the Betti and Franchi families, lived and laboured in troublous times, and proved himself a firm friend of the Medici. His epitaph in the Church Degli Angeli, Florence, assures us that his life was spent *sine ullâ avaritiâ aut ambitione*. The text refers to the Dialogue called after Count Cesare Ercolano. Varchi's principal work was the " Storia Florentina " (16 books 1523-37): he was an indefatigable sonnetteer, his productions numbering 958 ; and his collected " Opere " fill two volumes large 8vo ; Trieste, Lloyd Austriaco, 1858.

[3] Celio Calcagnino, of Ferrara (died in 1541), wrote chiefly upon antiquities and classical subjects : his works are now more quoted than read.

*Lyricks*                                    C

⁴ Rhodiginus (*i.e.*, of Rovigo) : Ludovicus Celius Ricchieri, born circ. 1450. He was protected by François I. during the Italian troubles, and he is supposed to have died broken-hearted after the Battle of Pavia. He left "Antiquarum Lectionum Libri xvi." (Venice, 1516; Paris, 1517); his life was written by Camillo Silvestri (Raccolta Calogera. IV. p. 157), and he is mentioned in the "Storia" of Tiraboschi (Vol. VIII. Part II. p. 225).

⁵ Dante so defines poetry in his famous philosophico-metrical Treatise "De Vulgari Eloquio." It has been introduced to the English public by the late Dante Gabriel Rossetti, painter and poet.

"Rhythmus," says Aristoxenus of Tarentum, a high authority quoted by Dr. Francis Hueffer ("The Troubadours," etc.; London, Chatto and Windus, 1878), "is the division of time into equally recurring parts longer and shorter (*i.e.* quantity), made perceptible to certain metrical movements (τὸ ρυθμιζόμενον"). In music it is the notes of a melody (μέλος); in dancing, bodily gesture (σωματικὴ κίνεσις); and in poetry, diction (λέξις). The weaker part of the metre was originally called ἄρσις when the voice or the foot was raised (*arsis est elevatio*); and the stronger was θέσις, when the tone fell as the dancer trod the ground (*thesis est depositio vocis ac remissio*). The terms have frequently changed meaning, and in Latin they were applied not to quantity, but to that rhetorical accent,—as in

Dies iræ, dies illa—

which by slow degrees overcame its rival, and led to the development of "Rhyme" or "Rime" proper. The latter was known to Homer and Horace, but the rhythmical principle prevented its development. *

⁶ Little need be said concerning Bembo, the Platonist and Petrarchist (born in 1470), who was made a Cardinal *malgré*

---

\* Nil satis est pulchra esse poëmata : dulcia sunto
Et quocumque volent animum auditoris agunto.

II Epist., III. 99, 100.

So I Odes, I. 2, 3. Meum + Olympicum : I Odes, VIII. 4, 5. Solis + militaris and many others.

*lui*, and who consoled himself with Poetry—partly amorous.
His portraits show a marked Hebrew face, much resembling
the late Sir Charles Napier (of Sind). His works fill 12 vols.
8vo (Milano, Soc. Tipograf. de' Classici Italiani, 1808); and his
"Rime" (Venice, 1530) are still read.

⁊ The assertion is over-hasty. Fr. Bernardo de Brito's
"Chronica de Cister" (Lib. VI. Cap. 1, m. fol. 372) quoted
Hendecasyllabics by Gonçalo Hermigues (circa 1090) before
Count Henrique had entered Portugal. A hundred and seventy
years afterwards D. Diniz (King Dennis, or Dionysius), who
was born three or four years before Dante (A.D. 1265), wrote
many Hendecasyllabics, and presumably Tercets. In the Dedi-
catory of his "Chronica Geral de Hispanha" (printed at
Valencia, 1546), Pedro Antam Beuter states that a certain
Mossen Jordi, who flourished about 1250, composed sonnets,
Sextines and *Tercecroles*, which are Tercets; moreover, that he
borrowed this form from older rhymers, such as the Hohen-
staufen Emperor Friedrich II. and his son Enzio (11th
century). Beuter quotes the following verses by Jo     —

> *E no he pace, e no tinch quim guarreig :*
> *Vol sobrel Cel, e non movi di terra :*
> *E no estrench res, etot la man abrás :*
> *Hoy he de mi, e vull altri gran bé,*
> *Si no amor, dons aço que sem ?*
> (There be be no Peace, yet have I none to war ;
> O'er Heaven I fly and never fare from Earth ;
> And nought hold I, yet all the world embrace :
> I hate myself and love another well,
> If that n'is Love then what bin it I feel ?)

The idea is thus borrowed by Petrarch :—

> *Pace non trovo, e non ho da far guerra*, etc.
> (Peace find I not, and may I not make war.)
>
> 1 Sonnet, Part I. 90.

From Petrarch it was imitated, or rather translated, by
Camoens, whose Sonnet IX. begins :—

> *Tanto de meu estado me acho incerto*, etc.

C 2

And, after all, the germ may be found in the "Amo et odi" of Catullus.

[8] Arnaut Daniel (Arnaldo Daniello), of Ribeyrac, the famous poet and musician, Troubadour and Joglar (*jocularius*) of the 12th century, from whom Dante borrowed the structure of sundry stanzas, and whom Petrarch ("Triumphs of Love," Cap. IV.) entitles "Gran maestro d'amor." He died after a very accidented life in A.D. 1189.

[9] Mandriale (Madriale, Madrigale, Madrigal) derives from the Greek, Ital. and Span. *Mandra* or *Mandria*, a flock or fold. Antonio da Tempo (p. 139, edit. Guion) adds, "A Mandra pecudum et pastorum, quia primò modum illum rithimandi et cantandi habuimus ab ovium pastoribus." Menage quotes the French Mandre (sheepfold), and deduces it from ἄντρον, a cave; I prefer to consider it a congener of the Arab. Mandarah (Manzar), a look-out place, adopted by the Sicilian Greeks from their "Semitic" (Arabian) neighbours. The oldest Madrigals were of two kinds, "Mandriales Communes" and "Mandriales cum retornellis," *i.e.* caudati, cowee'd with single lines, or with couplets. Carducci (Studi Litterari) notes that the Madrigal should conserve its old simplicity:—"Un eco di beliti ci si aveva sempre a sentire, ma per benino, in guisa che assomigliasse a un sospiro dell' anima." The Portuguese "Villancete" is the Spanish *Villancico*, a song of "Villeins," or peasants.

[10] Rengifo (Juan Diaz), Professor of Grammar and Rhetoric, whose "Arte Poética Española" (Salamanca, 1592, 4to), treats of the technique of the older Castilian composition and of the Italian innovations due to Boscan and Garcilasso. For ample details see Bouterwek (Eng. Trans. p. 103 seq.), and Vol. III. p. 265, etc., "History of Spanish Literature," by George Ticknor; London, Trübner, 1863.

[11] The Canzon was affected by Guido Guinicelli the Bolognese, who flourished in the early 13th century, before Dante's day. Longfellow (Dante, II. 304, Tauchnitz edit.) quotes Rossetti's translation of his most famous production, a Canzon on the Nature of Love, which won high praise from the Author of the Commedia (Purg., XXVI. 9c-1co). Of his

life little is known. In Appendix I. the reader will find further notices of the Canzon.

[12] Vincentio Cartario or Cartari (Vincentius Cartarius), a
now forgotten archæologue of the 16th century. It may here
be noted that certain mediæval writers looked upon Mercury,
with his wings and his functions, as the "Angel" of Jupiter ;
the same was the case with Iris.

[13] Onciacus, or Onciatus, Guillaume d'Oncieu, a French
writer of repute on Jurisprudence. Besides the "Decas" (1
vol. 8vo, 1584) he wrote eight works duly enumerated in that
portable publication, "Grosses Universal Lexicon," von J. H.
Zedler, Leipzig und Halle, 1740, in 64 vols. folio.

[14] Surrupita alludes generally to a common defect in sonnet-
writing where the subject is left incomplete and the reader
remains in expectancy, as it were, of what the writer is about
to say. He may refer especially to a sonnet of his contemporary, Antonio Ferreira, beginning :—

O' olhos, donde Amor suas frechas tira, etc.

(Eyne! from whose depths Love shoots his shafty showers.)

This first of the quatorzaine, addressed to a pair of eyes, is
followed by the contents of the Sonnet forming a mere string of
exclamations and adding nought to its object. The second
Tercet should have predicated the subject, as Camoens shows in
two "continued Sonnets" (Nos. XXXV. and CXXXVIII.). Surrupita was a distinguished sonneteer, and, as will appear, may have
a right to claim some of the 360 (e.g., Nos. CXVI. and CCIX.)
which bear the name of Camoens. His works "Poesias e Prosas
ineditas de F. R. L. Soropita," with Preface and Notes, were
published by Snr. Camillo Castello Branco at Oporto, in 1868.
In Camoens' day, however, the "little sound" was a general
favourite, and almost all educated Portuguese seem to have
written Sonnets.

[15] Under "Odes" the Prologist would here include Canzons
and Sextines. Fernando de Herrera (1500–1578, which
Ticknor makes 1597) was an ecclesiastic of Seville, in whose
honour Cervantes wrote a Sonnet. His learned and voluminous
Commentary on Garcilasso appeared in 1580. Amongst his

many works were a poem on the Battle of Lepanto, Don John of Austria being one of his favourite heroes ; and an Ode on the defeat and death of Dom Sebastiam. His unpublished Eclogues are lost ; his other writings were brought out (1619) by his friend Francisco Pacheco, the painter, with a preface by Rioja. He was a lover of the (Petrarchian) "sonetto," which he declared to be " the most beautiful form of composition in Spanish and Italian poetry, and the one which demands the most art in its construction and the greatest grace " (Ticknor).

[16] Petrarch wrote nothing which he entitled " Elegies," or funeral odes; but his *Trionfi*, composed in terza rima, are purely elegiac. In some editions of his works (e.g., that of Naples, 1609, 16mo) a short poem in Tercets entitled *Capitulo*, possibly by the printers, is also an elegy, beginning :—

*Nel cor pien di amarissima dolcezza*, etc.

(Within a heart which brims with bitterest sweet.)

[17] To Sannazaro and Rota the Prologist might have added Lodovico Paterno in Italy, and the unrivalled Garcilasso in Spain. Rota (born in 1409 and died in 1575) was a Neapolitan of knightly family, who wrote much Latin verse and a Canzoniere (Song-book) of some celebrity. His fame rests upon his "Egloghe Piscatorie," which number fourteen (1 vol. 12mo, 104 pp.) : their nobility of style, harmonious proportions and graceful execution have entitled their author the " Sannazaro of Halieutics." The favourite metre is the hendecasyllabic with half-lines, as in the Canzon. Camoens seems to have read Rota, judging from such passages as :—

O Cimodoce, o Deto, o Panopea

[18] " Hispanha " here including Portugal. The " Grosa," now written " Glosa," means primarily a gloss proper, secondarily a short poetical composition after the manner of impromptus. The " Volta," etymologically signifying a turn, a Ritornelle, a song with a " bob " or burden, will be noticed at full length in a future page. The author is hardly justified in saying that the Glosa is peculiar to the Iberian Peninsula : Italy knows nothing older than the popular Stornello. And he is certainly incorrect when he makes the " Verso pequenho," or

octosyllabic line, proper to Spain." Not to mention the Iambic Dimeter of the Greeks and Romans, the Celtic Bards carefully cultivated this measure, which they adorned with rhyme, and, in this matter, they set the example to Southern Europe.

[19] Gregorio Sylvestre deserves this praise as a writer of octosyllabic "Glosas." A Portuguese, born in Lisbon and brought up in Spain where his life was spent, he treated many other subjects in "short verse," and he shared popularity with Garci Sanchez de Badajoz; Bartholomeu de Torres Naharro; D. Juan Fernandez de Heredia, and Christoval de Castillejo. His works were printed in Lisbon by Manuel de Lyra (12mo, 1592), and at Granada by Sebastiam de Mena (1 vol. 8vo).

[20] This again is supposed to allude to Antonio Ferreira, a rhymer charged with using redundant words ; with ignoring the ἐπφωνια, which Quinctilian calls "Vocalitas"; and with not satisfying the conditions of Aristotle ("De A. P.," Cap. i.) concerning imitation, harmony and number. The same critique might apply to Diogo Bernardes, the "sweet singer of the Lima" (Almeida Garrett), and to his contemporary, Pedro Andrade Caminha.

[21] As will be seen, opinions differ upon this subject (Appendix I. § 2).

[22] The sentence was thus printed by the Prologist in his first edition. In the second, however, the friends of Manoel Correa, who wrote a meagre study of Camoens and his Epos (see "Camoens, his Life and his Lusiads," Vol. I. p. 109), had the words changed to "Tratar do estylo Heroico nam he deste lugar ; porque o Licenciado Manoel Correa, que está commentando suas Lusiadas, terá esse cuidado." Note the change of "Lusiada" to "Lusiadas."

[23] Camoens, in his Eclogues as in his Epic, imitated Virgil rather than the greater master of Pastoral Poetry—Theocritus. Hence his Bucolics, Agreutics and Halieutics are held to be pitched in too high a key, and the reproach is especially levelled at Numbers 1, 2 and 6.

[24] Carvilius Pictor, alias the Grammarian, wrote the celebrated Æneidomastix according to the Pseudo-Donatus, "Vita Virgil.," p. 62.

²³ Petrus Crinitus : "De Poetis Latinis," etc., Libri I I. (Florence, 1505). He composed Carmina and many other works duly catalogued by Grässe, Part III. pp. 754–878.

²⁶ Manoel de Faria y Sousa, the Arch-Commentator, who will often be mentioned (Appendix I.), was scandalised by the evident faultiness of the Editio Princeps. With incredible diligence and immense labour he collated the various copies of Camoens' Works ("Camoens : his Life and his Lusiads," I. 107). Throughout his four folios he constantly alludes to his Commentary on the Redondilhas (roundels), Glosas and Voltas. The manuscript must have been well known in the early part of this century ; the Didot edition (Paris, 1815) mentions it as "existing in the Library of the R. Convent, Na. Sa. da Graça of Lisbon," and indeed the Editor, by favour of the Librarian, had leave to copy from it (Vol. IV., Prolog. p. vi.) Report says that when Monastic Orders were abolished, the MSS. in three vols. found their way to the Central Depot, Sam Francisco da Cidade. At my request a friend, D. Eduardo Vanzeller, made inquiries for these papers which I am anxious to have published : unfortunately the search failed, and we find reason to fear a final disappearance. I cannot but blame the Committee of Management for the Camoens Centenary (1880) : a vast mass of matter, mostly rubbish, was printed, whilst nothing was done to rescue from oblivion the valuable legacy left by the Arch-Commentator. *

²⁷ The "Court" is Lisbon in Portugal, Madrid in Spain.

---

\* F. y S. died in the house of the Marquess de Montebello, Madrid, and the autopsy showed liver-disease. The learned Viscount Juromenha writes that the library of the Duke de Villa Hermosa (Madrid) may contain, and in fact he has heard that it does contain, certain MSS. of the Arch-Commentator. He justly observes "quem quer vai" ; but the venerable Editor has not yet found an opportunity.

---◇---

# SONNETS.

# LYRICKS OF CAMOENS.

— •:• —

## I.

*Em quanto quis Fortuna que tivesse*
(General Proposition or Proëmium of Rhythmas, Petrarch, I. 1).

While Fortune willèd that for me be dight
   Some grateful Esperance of some glad Content,
   The gust of loving Thought a longing lent
To pen its pleasures and its pains to write:
But Love, in terror lest my Writ indite
   Lere for the judgment he hath never shent,
   So with his darkling pains my Genius blent
That mote I never tell his tale of sleight.

O ye, whom Love's obligeance may subjèct
   To Wills so divers! when you read thereof
   Bound in one Booklet cases so diverse;
(Which all be truthful, facts without defect)
   Learn that according as you have the Love,
   So shall you have the Lore, of this my verse.

## II.

*En cantarey de Amor taõ docemente,*
(Particular Proëm of the Love-songs, Petrarch, I. 87).

My song of Love I will so sweetly sing,
  In such fair concord of concerted phrase,
  That twice a thousand chances Love displays
Shall breasts unmovèd with emotion wring.
I'll so do Love new Life to all shall bring,
  Limning nice secrets in a thousand ways,
  Soft angers, sighs that yearn for bygone days,
Foolhardy Daring, Absence and her sting.

Yet, Ladye! of that honest open scorn
  Shown by your eye-glance, blandly rigorous,
  I must content me saying minor part:
To sing the graces which your geste adorn,
  Your lofty composition marvellous,
    Here lack me Genius, Lere, and Poet-art.

## III.

*Com grandes esperanças ja cantey,*
(Petrarch, I. 144-145; also Pietro Bembo).

Whilere I sang my song with hope so high
  Might win the godheads in Olympus-wone;
  Then for my singing 'gan I weep and moan,
And now for weeping yet again weep I.
When viewed my Past with meditative eye
  Costs me the memory such high price, I own
  That grief of seeing griefs so woebegone
Is greatest grievance of my griefs gone by.

Then, if 'tis clear that whatso Ills torment me
  Must gar increasèd other Ills torment,
Now can I never hope that aught content me.
  But is this only Fancy's False that shent?
O feckless Vision, idle Thought that blent me!
  What! I, e'en I, can hope to see Content?


## IV.

*Despoys que quis Amor que eu só passasse*
(The pains and inquietude of love.   Cf. Canz. X.).


When Love so willed on me alone be vented
  What Ills for many had reparted He,
  He made me Fortune's thrall, for He could see
No more that mote in me be represented:
She, that her gain from Love should be augmented,
  In pains he only doomèd me to dree,
  What for none other wight consented she,
Gave her consentment be for me invented.


Lo! here with various song fare I complaining,
Copious and exemplaire for one and all,
Subject to serve this Tyrant tway's behest,
My various madness in my verse constraining,
Sad whoso straighteneth in such guise his Rest,
And rests contented with a boon so small!

## V.

*Em prisoens baxas fuy hum tempo atado;*
(He laments the loss of his loved ancilla).

I lay in Durance vile long while detainèd,
  The shameful quittance of my faults to pay :
  E'en now my fetters drag I on my way,
The chains by Death, to my despight, unchainèd :
I sacrificèd life to cares unfeignèd,
  For Love ne'er loveth steer or lamb to slay :
  Exiles I saw, saw misery, saw dismay ;—
Meseems this hapless Life was so ordainèd.

I waxt contented with small mercies, knowing
  That such Contentment were but shame to hend,
    Sole for the sighting what were life's delight.
But now my star (how well I see its showing !),
  And blinding Death, and Chance of dubious end,
    Made me all pleasures view with naught but
      fright.

## VI.

*Ilustre, e digno Ramo dos Meneses,*
(To D. Fernando, en route for Red Sea ?).

Illustrious Scion of the tree Meneses !
  To whom large-handed, all-providing Heaven
  (Which kens not erring) heritage hath given,,
To crush the harness which the Moor encases :
Despising Fortune, spurning her mismazes,
  Go whither Fate shall guide you foewards driven :
  On Erythrèan deeps light fiery leven,
And be new splendour to the Portugueses.

Lay with firm Will, with forceful Breast abate
The insolent Pyrat, till Gedròsia dread
 And quake the classic Taprobanian shore.
Cause of new tincture lend the Arabian Strait
 So may the Red Sea front henceforth be red,
 Reddened with glowing of the Turk-man's gore.

## VII.

*No tempo que de Amor viver soïa,*
(The inconstancies of his youth. Cf. Canz. II. 6; VIII. 2).

When love, love only, was my daily diet,
 I fared not always iron'd to oar and chain;
 (Nay) tied at times and then untied again,
In various flames with varied Passions' riot.
Willed not that single flame my heart disquiet
 The Heavens, so mote I hard experience gain
 No change of cause in lover-care is fain
To work a changing of my Fortune's fiat.

And if awhile I fared fancy-free,
 'Twas like the wight who rests for breathing sake
Till with more vigour to his tasks turn he.
Laud to the Love-god in my misery!
 Since for his pastime he was pleasèd take
This my so weary long-drawn agony.

## VIII.

*Amor, que o gesto humano na Alma escreve,*
(The sight of his lover's tears).

Amor, who human geste on Soul doth write,
  One day showed sparkles twain of lively Sheen,
  Whence-purest Chrystal poured in currents twin,
'Mid living Rose and Snow-plot virgin-white.
Mine eyes, that dared not trust them to such sight,
  For certifying what could there be seen,
  Were to a fount convèrt, which made my teen
Of easy sufferance and my load more light.

Love swears that softening Will and gentling Gree
  Gender the first effect, but then the Thought
Maddens the man who deems it verity.
  Look ye how Love hath in one moment brought
Fro' tears, which honest Pity setteth free,
  Tears with immortal satisfaction fraught.

## IX.

*Tanto de meu estado me acho incerto,*
(Petrarch, I. 90).

I find so many doubts my State enfold,
  I thrill in living lowe with trembling chill:
  Sans cause I laugh and tears conjointly spill;
I grasp at all the World and naught I hold:
Whatso I feel is of disordered mould:
  My soul outpoureth fire, my eyes a rill:
  Now gladly hope I, then despairs my Will:
Now Reason wanders, then grows calm and cold.

Being in Earth-Life unto Heaven I fly :
   Find in one hour one thousand years, natheless
     In thousand years I find no hour to claim.
If any ask me wherefore so fare I ;
   My answer is I know not, yet I guess
     'Tis but because I saw your sight, Madàme !


## X.

*Transforma se o amador na cousa amada,*
(He corrects a carnal thought.  Cf. Sonnet 31, Canz. I. 3).


Becomes the Lover to the Loved transmewèd,
   By thoughts and reveries the Fancy fire :
   Then have I nothing left me to desire,
For the Desirèd is in me enduèd.
If my transmewèd soul in her be viewèd,
   What can my formal body look for higher ?
   Only in self for Rest it can retire,
Since that same Spirit hath my form imbruèd.

But this half-goddess with fair purity fraught,
   As Subject dwells in Accident inlaid,
     So to this Soul of mine shows self conform ;
E'en as Idea fares she in my Thought ;
   While the pure lively Love whereof I'm made,
     Like unto simple Matter seeks its Form.

———

## XI.

*Passo por meus trabalhos tam isento*
(He wants more pain—ad majorem Amoris gloriam).

I through my travails pass so fancy-free
  Fro' Sentiment, or high or low its vein,
  That for the Love-will wherewithal I pain,
Love more of torture oweth to my fee.
But Love so slowly fareth slaying me,
  With Theriack tempering still his draught venene,
  His ordered pains ordained I disordain,
For-that my sufferings nill consent agree.

Yet, an such fineness lurk in Love's intent,
  Mine Ills with other Ills to pay pretending,
    This joyaunce melts me as Sol melts the Snow.
But an he view me so with Ills content,
  The Niggard grudgeth me his pains, intending
    The more he pays me, still the more he owe.

## XII.

*Em flor vos arrancou, de entaõ crecida,*
(Of Dom A. de Noronha slain at Ceuta).

In flower uprooted you, Bloom yet unblown,
  (Ah, Dom Antonio !), Fortune's dire decree,
    Where your brave arm display'd such bravery
That hath o'er past Renown oblivion thrown.
One single reason to my thought is known,
  Wherewith so care-full teen shall comfort see
    That if an honoured Death i' the world there be,
No larger life-tide could your Spirit own.

An hold my humble verse a verve so strong
   That to my heart-felt Hope respond my Art,
      You shall supply me theme of special Glory ;
And sung in long-drawn and in saddest song,
   If you were slain by hand of cruel Mart,
      You shall immortal live in mortal story.

## XIII.

*Num jardim adornado de verdura,*
(To Violante, the Violet, fair and pure).

Into a garden verdure-deckt and dight,
   Where varied flowers amelled floors of green,
   One day came pacing Love's own goddess-queen
With the Hunt-goddess whom the groves delight.
Diana straightway pluckt a Rose pure-white,
   Venus a Lily of the reddest sheen ;
   But far exceeding a' the lave were seen
The Violets clad in loveliness and light.

Both ask of Cupid, who stood nigh in stead,
   Which of those flowrets three he fainest take
   For suavest, purest, which the loveliest shows.
Then the Boy, slily smiling, this wise said,
   "They all be beauties, natheless I make
      Viola anteceding Lily, much more Rose !"

----

## XIV.

*Todo animal da calma reponsava,*
(Cry of Jealousy).

All animals rested in the Noontide still
　　Liso alone felt naught of midday-glow ;
　　For-that his respite from his lover-lowe
Lay in the Nymph he sought to allay his Ill :
Made every mountain-height to shake and thrill :
　　The triste complainings of his throe-full woe
　　But ne'er that hardened bosom ruth would show,
The willing Captive of another Will.

Now worn by wander 'neath the bosky shade,
For Memory sake, deep in a beechen bole,
He graved these words that told his misery :—
"𝔑one lay such flattering unction to his 𝔖oul
𝔄s trust in 𝔚oman's breast, which 𝔑ature made
𝔗o nothing constant save 𝔍nconstancy."

## XV.

*Busque Amor novas artes, novo engenho,*
(A Plaint of Love).

Devise Love novel arts, a new design
　　And novel-coy Disdains my life to slay ;
　　My lovely hopes he may not bear away,
He may not bear away what ne'er was mine.
Look on what pauper Hope I feed and pine !
　　See what security unsure of stay !
　　I fear no Warfare, Change hath no dismay
For ship-wreckt waif that swims the yeasty brine.

But albe Disappointment dwell no more
  Where Esperance faileth, there Love hides a care,
    An Ill that slayeth me withouten show.
Days were he pleasèd in my soul to store
  A what I know not, born I know not where,
    Comes why I know not, pains I know not how.


## XVI.

*Quem ve, Senhora, claro, e manifesto,*
(Ut vidi, ut perii ! Written for a friend ?).


Who seeth, Ladye ! clear and manifest,
  The lovely being of your eyën-light,
    Nor loseth seeing-faculty, seen their sight,
He nills pay duties owèd to your geste.
This seemed me honest price for such acquest ;
  But I, the better to deserve the right
    To love those eyne, paid more, my Life, my Sprite,
Hence naught remaineth in my hand for " rest."


Thus now my Soul, my Life, mine Esperance
  I gave you, everything that made me man :
    But all the interest I alone can show.
For 'tis such blessèd, such belovèd chance
  To give you all I have and all I can,
    The more I pay you, still the more I owe.

## XVII.

*Quando da bella vista, e dolce riso :*
(He sings her perfections—dulce ridentem).

While of your laughter sweet and lovely eyes
  My sight enjoyeth rarest nutriment,
  I feel so elevate my thought's Intent
That makes me see on Earth the Paradise.
I bin so parted from what Humans prize
  All other blessings deem I winds that went :
  Thus to this term arrivèd (such my sent),
He fares not far fro' where his Reason flies.

I pride me not, Madame ! on praise of you ;
  For of your graces whoso takes full range
    Must feel that man such knowledge never learns.
You are such strangeness for this world to view,
  Excellent Dame ! it may not seem us strange
    Who made you, made the Skies and made the
    Sternes.

## XVIII.

*Doces lembranças da passada gloria,*
(The Displeasures of Memory).

Delicious Memories of a Past so glorious,
  Reft by that robber Fortune's rage-full spleen ;
  Let me repose one hour in peace serene,
You gain fro' me small gains howe'er victorious.
Stampt on my Soul hold I the tale notorious
  Of this past welfare ; had it never been,
  Or being had never past ! but now my teen
In me leaves nothing save its trace memorious.

I live on memory-fare, and die forgot
　　By her whose memory should have held me fast,
　　Had she remembered state of such Content.
O that return to birth had been my lot !
　　Well had I learnt to enjoy my happy Past,
　　If known what ills the Present can present.

## XIX.

*Alma minha gentil, que te partiste*
(On the death of his lover : the chef d'œuvre).

My gentle Spirit ! thou who didst depart
　　This life of Miscontent so sudden tane ;
　　Rest there eternal in the heavenly Reign,
Live I pent here to play sad mortal part.
If in that happy Home, where throned thou art,
　　Consent to memories of the Past they deign,
　　Forget not thou my love, whose ardent strain
Thou sawst in purest glance that spake my heart.

And if such love gain aught of grace fro' thee,
　　If aught avail this woe wherewith I pine,
　　This pining woe that knows no remedy ;
　　Pray Him who shorted those few years of thine,
So soon He bear me hence thy sight to see
　　As soon He bore thee fro' my sorrowing eyne.

———

## XX.

*Num bosque, que das Ninfas se habitava,*
(Sibella, or Belisa, and Cupid : a scherzo).

Deep in a woody, Nymph-inhabited dell
  Sybil, the fairest Nymph, fared forth one day ;
  And clomb a tree embrowning solar ray,
To pluck the golden bloom of asphodel.
Cupid who wont (and thus him aye befell)
  Noon in its sombre coolth to while away,
  His bow and bolts suspended to a spray,
Before he suffered Sleep his eyne compel.

The Nymph, observing such occasion suit
  For so great derring-do, no time delayeth ;
    But, tane the coy Lad's weapons, fares a-flying.
She bears his love-shafts in her eyes to shoot :
  Shun her, ye Shepherds ! fly, for all she slayeth,
    Save only me, who only live by dying.


## XXI.

*Os Reinos, e os Imperios poderosos*
(To D. Teodosio, Duke of Braganza.   Cf. Sonn. 227).

Royaumes and Empires highest in might and main
  Which grew to prowest pride of worldly place,
  Or bloomed and blossomèd by Valour's grace,
Or by their Barons strong in lettered vein :
Greece bare her famed Themistoclean strain ;
  Rome gat her greatness by the Scipian race ;
  Twelve Peers the glory-path for France did trace ;
Cids with the warlike Laras 'nobled Spain :

Unto our Portugal, that now meseems
  A breed unlikest olden breed to bear,
    Freedom and Fame gave they fro' whom you're
      sprung.
In you we sight (great Scion and latest Heir
  O' the State Braganzan!) thousand-fold extremes
    Peers to your blood, sans peers in years so
      young.

## XXII.

*De vós me aparto (O vida!) e em tal mudança*
  (First of eighteen parting-sonnets).

I leave you (dear my life!) and as I leave
  The very sense of Death-in-Life I feel;
  I weet not why we seek contenting Weal,
If more must lose who doth the more receive.
But this firm 'surance unto you I give,
  Albeit my tormentry this body kill,
  Thro' the dark waters of the Lethe-rill
Secure in Memory the dead Past shall live.

Better sans you mine eyes with woe be wet
  Than with another Light they shine content:
Better forget them you than they forget.
  Better with this remembrance be they spent,
Than by forgetting undeserve to get
  The glories won by pains they underwent.

## XXIII.

*Chara minha Enemiga, em cuja mão*
(First Sonnet to Dynamènè the drowned).

My fondest-hateful Foe! within whose hand
   Placed all my joys and joyaunce Aventùre;
   Failèd for thee on Earth a sepulture,
That fail me Comfort fro' my bosom bann'd:
Ocean for ever ever stole from land
   And won and joyed thy peregrine Formosure:
   But long as Being shall for me endure
Live in my spirit shall thy Form be scann'd.

And if my rustick verse such verve may vaunt
   That it may vow thee long historick tale,
     Of by-gone love so pure, so true to thee;
Thou shalt be ever celebrate in my chaunt:
   For long as mortal memory shall prevail
     My Script shall serve thee for Epitaphy.

## XXIV.

*Aquella triste, e léda madrugada,*
(Written when en route for Africa?).

That dawn of dewy Day, so black, so bright,
   O'ercharged with yearning pyne and pitiful woe
   Long as the world an after-grief shall know
I will that Day-dawn aye with Fame be dight.
Only she saw when brake her dappled light
   In air, illuming earth with clearest glow
   This Will the presence of that Will forego
Which ne'er had power such parting-tide to sight.

Only she saw the tears in beads distil
  From these and other Eyne, conjoint exprest,
And roll uniting in large-streamèd rill.
  Only she heard the words of yearning quest
Whose magick influence the fire could chill
  And to the damnèd Souls deal balmy rest.


## XXV.

*Se quando vos perdi, minha esperança,*
(Love forbids him to forget).


If, when I lost you, you mine Esperance !
  I had conjointly lost all memory-pow'r,
  Of the sweet Goods that fade and Ills that flow'r,
Scant had I grievèd for such change of chance.
But Love I cherisht in full confidence
  Would to me represent, with nicest lore,
  How oft he saw me 'joy the joyous hour
That such Remembrance work my Life offence.


By things that hardly left at most a sign
  For-that I gave them to forgetfulness,
I see my thought with memories overcast.
  Ah, my hard Planet ! ah the dire distress !
What can be greater Ill in evils mine
  Than the remembrance of such happy Past ?

## XXVI.

*Em fermosa Letëa se confia,*
(Some hidden application.   Ovid, Met. X. 68-71).

So did Lethæa for-that fair confide,
   Where mortal vanity doth show the way,
   From proud to confident she went astray,
And with the Gods of Heaven in beauty vied.
Better to hinder such career of pride,
   (For born are many errors of delay)
   The Gods resolved a penalty she pay,
For her foolhàrdise all their force defied.

But Olenus lost for Lethæa's sake,
   Whose love forbade him bear wi' patient heart
     On so much beauty chastisement so dread,
Willèd of alien sin the pains to take;
   Yet Love unwilling Death the twain depart,
     To a hard stone the Pair transfigurèd.

## XXVII.

*Males, que contra mim vos conjurastes :*
(Written during last days in India?   Cf. No. 33).

Ills ! that against my faring well conspire;
   How long shall 'dure you in your dure intent;
   If it endure that 'dure my chastisement,
Suffice to you the torments dealt your Ire.
But an ye persevere, for ye aspire
   To see the high-toned Thoughts of me forspent;
   Stronger the Cause that strength to bear them lent,
Than you that Being from such cause acquire.

And, as your purpose 'tis, when I'm a-mort,
   To end what Evils from these loves I dree,
      Bid of so long-drawn pains an end I view.
Thus (both contented) each shall hug his sort :
   You shall win victory by winning me,
      And I be winner being won by you.


## XXVIII.

*Estáse a Primavera trasladando*
(Her charms are those of Spring.   Written for a friend ?).


Prime all her beauties loveth to transmew
   In your delicious glance of modest hest ;
      Your lovely brow and lips and cheeks she drest
Wi' Lily, Pink, and Rose's mingled hue :
In sort, by shift of variegated view
   Nature in you her might shows manifest ;
      That Mount and Meadow, Stream and Wood attest
The love, my Ladye, they have vowed to you.

If now you nill that who hath lover-claim
   The fragrant fruitage of this flowerage cull,
      Soon shall those buds of grace abide forlorn :
Because it little booteth, fairest Dame !
   That Love with Lovelings sow your garden full
      If your condition breed but briar and thorn.

## XXIX.

*Sete annos de Pastor Jacob servia*
(Jacob, Rachel, and Leah: then a favourite theme).

Seven years a Shepherd, Jacob did obey
　Laban, the lovely sheep-maid Rachel's sire,
　Him served he not, he servèd her for hire
With one and only wish to win the May.
The days in esperance of a single day
　He passed, contented only her to admire,
　But Laban, cautious of a youth's desire,
In lieu of Rachel gave him Leah for pay.

When the sad Shepherd saw the snare and sleight
　That stole the Shepherd-maiden from his lot
　As though deservèd nought his long Desert;
To other seven-years' service self he dight,
　Saying:—"More had I served and slaved were not
　For so long loving Life-tide all too curt."

## XXX.

*Está o lascivo, e doce passarinho*
(He compares himself with the murdered bird).

Sits the sweet Birdie, ever gladsome-gay,
　His ruffled plumy robe wi' beaklet preening;
　And his soft lay sans measure, full of meaning,
Thrilleth in joyaunce from the rustick spray.
The cruel Birder, bent upon his prey,
　With stealthy footsteps comes fere purpose screening;
　And with sure aim the grided arrow gleening,
Speeds him on Stygian Lake to nest for aye.

This wise a heart, in freedom wont to wend
  (Albe for many a day predestinate)
    Was smit with Death-stroke where it saw no
      sign :
For the Blind Archer waited that at end
  He might advantage of my careless state,
    Deep ambushèd within your clearest eyne.


## XXXI.

*Pede o desejo, Dama, que vos veja :*
(After asking a mis-favour.  Cf. Sonn. 10 and 129: Canz. I. 3).

Desire, my Ladye ! all to see requireth :
  'Tis fooled and kens not whither 'twould aspire :
  This love so fine-drawn runs to thinnest wire,
Who sense it never know what it desireth :
There is in Nature naught but what suspireth
  For a condition permanent-entire ;
  To win desirèd things unwills Desire,
Lest naught remain whereto his will aspireth.

But this my pure Affection suffereth loss :
For as the heavy Stone hath aye for art,
In Nature's central gravity self to grave :
This wise my Thoughts and Fancies fro' the part
Which in my human flesh fares earthy-gross,
Made me, my Ladye ! such a fall to crave.

––––––

## XXXII.

*Porque quereys, Senhora, que offereça*
(Written before the Indian voyage?).

Why, Ladye ! would you see my life resign'd
　To bear so weighty Evils you design ?
　If you be wrath for that I be indign
He's to be born whom digne of you you'll find.
Intend, however much for you I've pin'd,
　I might be digne of prize that made me pine,
　But Love consents not such low price assign
To thoughts by lofty Lealty refine'd.

This wise no equal payment shall atone
　For all I suffered ; yet you owe it me
Who to bear such despight the power have shown.
And if the value all your wooers own
　Must equal yours, perforce this doom you'll dree,
To wone a-loving Self and Self alone.

## XXXIII.

*Se tanta pena tenho merecida*
(Continuing No. 32).

If I have merited such pain-full plight
　In pay of suffering so hard penalties ;
　Approve, Madame ! on me your cruelties,
Here hold you offered a self-doomèd sprite ;
Whereon experiment (an you deem it right)
　Disprize, disfavours and asperities ;
　For fiercer sufferings, in the firmest guise,
I'd bear right bravely in this life-long fight.

But what avails me against your eyes' pretence?
 To them all Foemen, will or nill, surrender ;
Yet I my heart will plant as shield to sense :
 For in such asperous Fray with force so slender
'Tis well that sithence I am sans defence
 I be mid couchèd spears my sole defender.

## XXXIV.

*Quando o Sol encuberto vay mostrando*
(Written at Ceuta ?    Petrarch, I. 90).

As Sol with veilèd brow his beams abasing
 Shows to the world Eve's gleaming gloaming light,
 Along a shore-land that delights the sight
I pace, my dearest foe in fancy tracing :
Here I beheld her plaited locks enlacing ;
 There hand supporting cheek so beauteous-bright ;
 Here gladly speaking, there all care-bedight ;
Now steadfast standing, now a-forwards pacing :

Here she was sitting, there she glanced at me
 Raising those ever fancy-freest eyne ;
 Here something startled, there again secure :
Here sat she saddenèd, there smilèd she
 And in these weary, wearing Thoughts, in fine,
 I lose vain Life-time which doth still endure.

## XXXV.

*Hum mover de olhos, brando e piadoso,*
(Her portrait.　Cf. Sonn. 78 and Ode VI. 1 6).

A soft and pity-full glancing of those eyes
　With naught to pity; a sweet Smile shame-represt
　As though enforced, a douce and gentle gest,
Doubting all worldly joys and vanities :
A quiet Energy hid in bashful guise.
　A modest favour and a gravest rest ;
　A purest Goodness, e'er the manifest
Index where pure and gracious Spirit lies :

A veilèd Daring; a retiring air ;
　A fear withouten fault ; a cheere serene ;
　　A long-drawn suffering with obedience fraught :
Such were the Beauties as the Heavens fair
　Of Circe mine, whose magick all venene
　　Had power to metamorphose all my Thought.


## XXXVI.

*Tomou-me vossa vista soberana*
(He boasts of being captured though fully armed).

Conquered and captured me your sovran Sight
　Where I had weapons handiest to my hand,
　That all who seek defence may understand
With those fair eyne foolhàrdise 'twere to fight
That mote her Victory rise to prower height,
　She first let Reason arm me with her brand :
　I thought to save me, but 'twas vainly plann'd,
For against Heaven avails not earthly Might.

If to your lot, withal, have promisèd
  Your lofty Destinies such victory,
Small gift they give you when all's done and said.
Then 'spite my standing on well-guarded stead,
  Yours be the Boast and Brave of conquering me,
And mine a greater by you conquerèd.


## XXXVII.

*Não passes, Caminhante.   Quem me chama?*
(To the Memory of D. Joam de Castro?).


Pass me not, Passer-by!—"Who names my name?"
  A novel Memory never heard before
  Of one who changèd life, a finite store,
For infinite, divine and clearest Fame.
"Who is 't so gentle praises doth acclaim?"
  One who ne'er doubted all his blood to outpour,
  Following the noble flag he ever bore,
Captain of CHRIST he loved with single aim.

Most blessèd sacrifice, most blessèd ending,
To God and Man in offering resign'd!
I will aloud proclaim a Sort so high.
Thou canst tell larger tale to all mankind,
Clear sign he ever gave through life a-wending
He would deserve such holy Death to die.


---

## XXXVIII.

*Fermosos olhos, que na idade nossa*
(Written for a friend ?).

Beautiful Eyën, to our days displaying
  Of high and heavenly Lore the surest sign,
  An ye would learn the power wherewith you shine,
Look on this creature of your own arraying !
You'll see how comes, the life o' me waylaying,
  That Smile which dealeth me this life of mine :
  You'll see for no more gifts o' Love I pine
The more fleet Time flits by, our hearts dismaying.

And if, in fine, you'd see you in this sprite
  As in glass brightly-shining, there you'll see
    Likewise your Soul angelical-serene.
But sore I doubt me 'tis to unsee my sight
  You will not, Ladye ! see yourself in me.
    So lively pleasures giveth you my teen !

## XXXIX.

*O fogo que na branda cera ardia,*
(To a lady whose face was singed by a taper).

The Fire, who burning made soft wax a prey,
  Sighting the gentle face in Soul I sight,
  With other firing of Desire was dight
To reach the Lights that conquer lustrous Day.
And, as he flamèd with a twofold ray,
  His hot impatience put all shame to flight ;
  And with exceeding fervency of light
He flew to kiss you where his image lay.

Happy that Fire who so much boldness shows
  To quench his brenning and his torments dern,
By sight of one to whom Sol terror owes.
  With love, my Ladye! all the Elements yearn
For you, and even Fire inflames the snows
  Which burn our bosoms and our fancies burn.


## XL.

*Alegres campos, verdes arroredos,*
(Written on return to Cintra from India? Petrarch, I. Canz. 27).


Glad smiling Pastures, gay and greeny Glade,
  Clear, fresh-cool Waters, with your chrystalline flow
  (The view repeating in the waves below)
Which from the rocky heights the meads invade:
Cliffs, stark and barefaced, Mounts o' forest shade
  That such a disconcerted Concert show;
  Know you withouten sanction of my woe
No more by you mine eyes may glad be made.

And sith no more you see me as you saw,
  No more your growth of greenth delicious cheers,
    Nor waves that come fast flowing joyous flood.
In you I'll sow remembrances that gnaw,
  I'll water you with lamentable tears,
    And after-grief shall spring fro' by-gone Good.


E 2

## XLI.

*Quantas vezes do fuso se esquecia*
(Daliana, loving Silvio, is loved by Laurenio).

Oft as forgot her spindle woe-forlore
　　Daliana (bathed in tears her beauteous breast)
　　So oft by asperous terror was opprest
Laurenio, losing hues of health he wore.
She, who loved Silvio than herself far more,
　　E'er sought to see him yet e'er failed her quest,
　　How, then, shall heal another heart's Unrest
Who can so illy Rest to self restore?

He, clearly trowing the so bitter truth,
　　With sobs exclaimèd, (while the treën shade
Inclined to hear his pyne and yearn for ruth)
　　How can be Nature so disorderèd
That with such different Will the twain indue'th
Whom Will of Fortune so conforming made?

## XLII.

*Lindo, e sutil trançado, que ficaste*
(To a lady who gave him a fillet in lieu of hair-lock).

Fair-woven Fillet! in whose pledge I find
　　Promise of remedy I desire to gain,
　　If sole the seeing thee so mad my brain,
What would the tresses erst by thee confine'd?
Those golden-huèd locks thou hast entwine'd,
　　That hold the solar splendours in disdain,
　　I weet not was't to make my prayer in vain,
Or if to find me them thou didst unbind.

Thee, fair-wove Fillet ! I in hand see hent
  And for the solace to my sorrows owed,
    Lacking that other I must take this dole :
And, if my longings may not win Content,
  I have to assure her 'tis in Love's own code
    A part must take who cannot take the whole.


## XLIII.

*O Cisne quando sente ser chegada*
(He sings the Swan-song ; for Natercia married ?).


The Swan, who feeleth that enfated hour
  Nigh draw and show him term of life draw nigh,
    A voice more touching, of more harmonie
Raiseth awaking lone deserted shore.
Fain he'd enjoy of life-tide something more,
  And mourneth weeping an unwilled good-bye :
    In yearning sorrow, for that dight to die,
His notes the Journey's mournful close deplore.

Thus I, my Ladye ! when to me was shown
  The tristful dying of my Love-in-grief,
    Already thinnèd to the thinmost thread ;
With suaver accent, more harmonious tone,
  Of your disfavours I to sing was lief,—
    " *Your faith perjurious and my Love done dead.*"

## XLIV.

*Por os raros estremos que mostrou,*
(In praise of four maids of honour).

For rare extremes displayed in days of yore,
   Pallas for learnèd, Venus for-that fair,
   Dian for chaste, Juno for queenly air,
Africk, Europa, Asia did adore.
He who conjoinèd by Almighty Pow'r
   Spirit and Flesh in generous league to pair,
   This World-machinery, lustrous 'yond Compare,
Fabrick'd with simple Elementals four.

But Nature willèd greater marvel see
In you, my Dames! when joined in every one
What she had portionèd amid her fours.
To you their splendours yielded Sol and Lune :
You with live light, and grace and purest blee,
Air, Earth, Fire, Water served as servitours.

## XLV.

*Tomava Daliana por vingança*
(Continues No. 41).

Willèd Daliana wed, to avenge the slight
   Of the hard Shepherd loved in love so true,
   With neatherd Giles ; and self-avenging rue
That alien error, false and coy despight :
The sure discretion and confiding light
   Which on her cheeks the rosy tincture drew,
   Wan Melancholy changed in every hue ;
For asperous Change oft changeth bright for blight.

Graciousest Floret laid in land so lean ;
   Sweet fruitage harvested by horny hand !
     Memories of other love and perjùred fay
Have turned to horrid hill the grassy green ;
   While cogging interest, feigning Love's command,
     Made even Beauty wend on hapless way.


### XLVI.

*Graõ tempo ha já que soube da Ventura*
(A Plaint written in India?).


Long Syne now 'tis sin' taught me Aventùre
   The life my fatal fiat hath forecast ;
   For such prolonged experience of my Past
Gave of my Future indice clear and sure :
Love fere and cruel ! Fortune aye obscure !
   Well have you tried me, bound me hard and fast :
   Lay waste, destroy, allow no weal to last ;
Do vengeance on my days that still endure.

Love wot from Fortune none to me befell
   And, that I feel the more what failures are,
He made my maintenance Dreams impossible.
   But you, my Ladye ! since (you see) my Star
None other wills, deign in my Soul to dwell,
   Where Fortune lacketh might to make or mar.

## XLVII.

*Se sómente hora alguma em vos piedade*
(Written after parting and en route to India?).

If I some hour some ruth in you could see
   Vouchsafed for so long torment to me dight,
   Love sore had suffered I depart the sight
Of those loved Eyes, long yearned-for Pyne of me !
From you I parted, but my volunty,
   Which like the natural limns you in my Sprite,
   Makes me this absence view in lying light,
Yet come I soon to prove that truth it be.

I *must* go, Ladye ! but in parting shed
   Sad tears shall ever claim revenge in kind
From eyes whereof you were the daily bread.
Thus to my pains I'll give Life torturèd ;
   For here, in fine, my Sovenance shall find
Myself in your oblivion sepulchrèd.

## XLVIII.

*Oh como me se alonga de anno em ano*
(One of the last, written at Mozambique?).

Ah me ! how longsome lengthens year by year
   This weary way-worn pilgrimage of mine !
   How shortens, flying to its fatal fine,
This my brief human course, this vain career !
With days decreasing increast Ills draw near ;
   I lost what cure I had, last anodyne :
   If-that experience teacheth to divine,
Each greater Hope doth greater snare appear.

I run to catch this welfare sans a chance;
  Welfare that faileth me in middle way,
And thousand falls destroy my confidence.
It flies, I tarry; and in tarriance
  When raised mine eyes to see if still it stay,
'Tis lost to vision and to esperance.

## XLIX.

*Já he tempo já, que minha confiança*
(A variant of No. 48; Horace, I. Odes, v.).

'Tis time, time 'tis that this my confidence
  Descend from heights of false opinion;
  But Love to Reason-rule will not be won;
I may not, therefore, with all Hope dispense:
Life, yes! for shift to asperous circumstance
  Forbiddeth length of life to hearts fordone,
  In Death hold I my sole salvation?
Yes! but who seeks for Death ne'er finds the chance.

Parforce I hope and eke parforce I live.
  Ah Love's hard Law that never deigns relent,
Nor soothes the Spirit which must captive grieve!
  But if, in fine, parforce to live I'm meant,
Wherefore want I the glory fugitive
  Of a vain Hope whose pain's my punishment?

———

## L.

*Amor, com a esperança já perdida*

(A variant of the last variant).

Amor ! with Esperance now for aye forlore,
    I pilgrimagèd to Thy sovran Fame ;
    And for my shipwreck-sign on stormy Main
In lieu of garments Life for offering bore.
What more of me wouldst Thou, who evermore
    Destroydst the Glory 'twas my boast to gain ?
    Deem not to conquer me, nor I again
Intend to enter by an issueless door.

Here seest thou life and soul and esperance,
    The sweet despoilings of my bygone weal,
    As long as willèd she, whom I adore.
On these thou lief mayst wreak thy vengeance,
    And, if determined more revenge to deal,
    Suffice thy heart-desire the tears I pour.

## LI.

*Apolo, e as nove Musas discantando*

(Petrarch, I. 12 and 47).

'Mid the nine Muses' choir Apollo singing
    To his gilt lyre, so influencèd my sprite
    With dèscant sweet, harmonical delight,
I hent in hand my pen and writ, beginning :—
"Happy the day, the hour, the moment bringing
    Those delicate eyne my very me to smite :
    Happy the feelings that could feel them dight
To die, with love-desires the heart unstringing."

This wise I sang when Cupid changed my chance
Whirling the wheel of Esperance, that raced
So legier, well nigh 'twas invisible.
For me the blackest night clear Day o'ercast;
And if remained me aught of Esperance,
'Twould be of balefuller bane—if possible.

## LII.

*Lembrancas saudosas, se cuidays*
(Cf. Sonn. 4 and 46).

Sad yearning Memories ! an ye still be straining
   To end my life-tide placed in such estate,
    I live not so ensnared by ban and bate,
As one not hoping more, far more, of paining.
Long time already you my heart are training
   To wone of whatso welfare desperate :
    Now I with Fortune have deliberate
To suffer torments of your own ordaining.

Patience I'll bind, as thole-pin bindeth oar,
   To what displeasures Life may lief affy :
    Let Thought as wills it care of suffering take.
For sith resistance can avail no more
   In such a cruel fall fro' height so high,
    Upon my sufferings I my fall must break.

## LIII.

*Apartavase Nise de Montano,*
(Of Nisé or Ines, the drowned Dame).

Departed Nisé parted from Montane,
   And, parting, ever woned within his sprite,
   For her in Memory limned the Shepherd-wight,
The freaks of Fortune easier to sustain.
Upon a Fore-land facing Indick main
   Propt on his curvèd crook he bowed his height,
   And o'er the vasty seas prolonged his sight,
Eyeing the wavelets reckless of his pain.

Since to such after-longings, pangs so fell,
   (Quoth he) would leave me she I most adore,
   I call to witness all the stars and spheres :
But, Waves, if aught of ruth in you may dwell
   Eke bear away the tears these eyelids pour
     E'en as you bear her that has caused the tears.

## LIV.

*Quando vejo que meu destino ordena,*
(Following No. 47).

Whenas I see my Destiny ordain,
   By way of proving, I from you depart,
   Leaving my welfare's better, higher part
That prove the very fault my bitterest bane :
The dure displeasure, dooming constant pain
   When musing Memory communes with my heart,
   Hardens my senses with such cunning art
That Absence-dolour grieves with lesser strain.

But how can hap it that a Change, destroying
    All that I fondest love, so far forbore
      To end my days, of parted life bereaving?
I'll bit and bridle this so bitter coying:
    For parting, Ladye! me had grievèd more
      Had I in parting grieved with lesser grieving.


## LV.

*Despoys de tantos dias mal gastados*
(Another sigh over the Past. Cf. Sonn. 49, and Petrarch, I. 48).


After so many days spent evilly,
    After so many a sleepless night spent ill,
    After so many a weeping tears in rill,
Vain sighs so many vainly sighed by me:
How did not Disenchantment set you free
    (Desires!) that of Forgottens, will or nill,
    You can a cure apply to wounds that kill,
Love cure-less made, and Time and Destiny?

Now had ye not so long experience
    Of Love's unreasons, whom you served amain,
In you resistance were a weak pretence.
    But, as for bane of you you bore Love's bane,
Time never cured, nor Absence-term immense,
    What hope ye (sad Desires!) of Love to gain?

## LVI.

*Nayades, vôs que os rios habitays,*
(A conceit: written in Coimbra?).

Naiads! ye ladyes who in rivers wone
And pour your treasures o'er the pined-for Plain,
Fain shall ye see these eyelids rail and rain
Waters that well-nigh equal all your own.
Dryads! who busk ye and with shafts are boun
  To fell the roe-deer in their flying slain,
  You shall see other Eyne like triumphs gain
O'er hearts of higher value felled and thrown.

Quit then your quivers and your waters cold;
  And haste ye, lovely Nymphs! if so incline'd
  To see one pair of Eyes breed many ills.
Here shall ye note how vain the days have roll'd:
  And yet not vainly note, for you shall find
  Her eyes your quivers hold, mine eyes your rills.

## LVII.

*Mudaõse os tempos, mudaõse as vontades;*
(Written perhaps in India).

Times change, change mortal loves and volunties;
  Changeth man's fortune, changeth confidence:
  The world is made of endless Change immense,
Ever assuming strange new qualities.
Continuous novelties our sight espies,
  From all we hopèd showing difference:
  Long live our sorrows graved in Memory-sense,
Our joy (if joy have been) in yearning dies.

Time clothes the country with a greeny coat,
  That erst lay clothed in snow-sheet hoar and frore ;
Time shifts my sugrèd lay to bitter note.
  And more than every day hath change in store,
Time works another Change of more dismay,
  For now as wont Time changeth never more.


## LVIII.

*Se as penas com que Amor taõ mal me trata*
(Exhorting her "carpere diem").


If pains whereby Love wreaks me such despight
  Permit me life so long to live by pain,
  Till seen those starry Eyne in wanness wane,
Whose sight doth slay me by their burning light :
And if long Time, who putteth all to flight,
  Wilt the fresh Roses that unpluckt remain,
  And if those tresses lose their lucent stain
Fram gold refinèd to fine silvern white :

Then, Ladye ! eke your sight shall see me changing
  The harrowing memory of your cruelties,
    When naught availeth you such change of chance.
With sighs you'll sight yourself o'er Bygones ranging,
  What time my power 'twill be to exercise
    On your too late regrets my vengeänce.

———

## LIX.

*Quem jaz no graõ Sepulchro, que descreve*
(Dialogue-sonnet on Dom Joam III.).

Who lies i' the lordly Tomb that doth indite
  So noble blazon on the doughty shield?
  "A Naught! for thus in fine all flesh must yield:
Yet did he all, held all that Mortal might."
A King?—"He did what Kings to do be dight:
  He studied Peace to practise, War to wield:
  But as on Moorman rude he weighed a-field,
So on his ashes, Earth! now lie thou light!"

Is't Alexander?—"Fancy no such thing!
More to conserve than conquer more he strave."
A Hadrian, holding Earth's dominion?
"More he observèd laws high Heaven gave."
Numa?—"No Numa he: 'tis John the King,
The Third of Portugal, seconded by none!"

## LX.

*Quem pode livre ser, gentil Senhora,*
(Petrarch, I. 75 and 16).

Who mote enjoy his freedom, Ladye fair!
  Seeing your presence with unprejudiced mind,
  If aye the Boy that was from babehood blind
Wone in the Babies which your pupils bear?
There reigns he, rules he, deals he love-doom thᵉᵉe
  There lives he venerate of all mankind;
  For the love-light, the features finely 'fined,
Are imaged idols for Love's worshipper.

Who sees the roses bloom on snows pure-white
　Set in the rondured, crispy threads of gold,
　　(If sight may haply through such lightning speer)
Sees aureate radiance, rays that pierce with light
　The dubious Spirit through the bosom's fold,
　　E'en as enpierceth Sol the chrystalline sphere.


## LXI.

*Como fizeste, ó Porcia, tal ferida ?*
("Dialogismus" to Portia Bruti).


How couldst, O Portia ! deal thee wound so dread?
　Was it free-willèd or was't innocence ?—
　"'Twas Love alone who sought experience,
How I could suffer Life by Death done dead."
And Love invited thine own blood to shed,
　Death to resist and make a Life-defence?
　"'Tis that my practice make I patience
Lest fear of dying do my Death impede."

Then wherefore swallow coals of burning lowe
　To steel self-customed ?—"'Tis that Love ordains
I die and, dying, pains of dying know."
　And art thou one that hurt of steel disdains ?
"Yea ! for we feel not an accustomed blow ;
　Nor would I Death withouten dying pains."

————

## LXII.

*Do taõ divino acento em voz humana,*
(To Joam José Leitam. Cf. Sonn. 134).

Of accents human yet in heavenly strains
    Of elegant phrase so singular-peregrine,
    My works (right well I weet) shall ne'er be digne ;
For my rude Genius disillusion deigns.
But from your choice illustrious Pen e'er drains
    Liquor excelling waters Caballine ;
    And by your aid shall Tage with flowrets fine
E'en Mantuan fulness fill with jealous pains.

And more, the Maidens of their meed unspare
    Born of that lovely dame, Mnemosyne,
To you their favours lent in world-known share,
    My Muse, and yours so famed for high degree,
Both in the world themselves may 'title rare,
    Yours for high Genius, mine for Jealousy.

## LXIII.

*Debaxo desta pedra está metido,*
(To Dom Fernando de Castro?).

Lieth ensepulchrèd beneath this stone,
    Resting fro' 'sanguined arms and fierce affrays,
    The illustrious Capitaine Fame loves to raise,
Fernan' de Castro, noble name all-known.
This, so much fearèd by all Orient fone,
    This, forcing Envy's self to sing his praise,
    This, who in fine held angry Mavors' rays,
To clay converted here shall ever wone.

Joy that thou breddest, warrior Lusitania !
  This Viriàtus born in other date,
    Nor less for ever o'er his loss lament.
Here for example take to thee Dardania ;
  For if one Brave could Roman braves abate,
    Yet stands not Carthage for this feat content.


## LXIV.

*Que vençays no Oriente tantos Reys ;*
(To Viceroy and Poet Dom L. de Athaide).


Than having conquered many an Eastern Roy ;
  Than having rendered back our Indick reign ;
    Than darkening every Fame man erst could gain
From Faithless peoples torn, with sore annoy.
Than conquering Death and Death's oblivious Loy ;
  And conquering all, in fine, that arms had tane ;
    More 'twas unarmed to conquer homely bane,—
Chimæras dire, and monster ills destroy :

Then upon conquering fone so fierce in bate,
And by your Derring-do so doing your name
Without a second heard a-world shall be ;
That which shall render you more worldly fame
Is that you conquer, Sir ! i' the friendly state,
Such lack of thanks, such jarring jealousy.

———

## LXV.

*Vossos olhos Senhora, que competem*
(Much admired).

Your eyes, my Ladye! that with Sol compete
   In Beauty's fervid sheen and clearest light,
   Full fill mine own with such a suave delight,
They melt in tear-floods when your sight they meet.
My Sense surrenders, prone before your feet,
   Blent in that presence of majestick might;
   And from drear dungeons tinct with òbscure night
Fear-fraught it only thinks to flit and fleet.

But an, perchance, your glance be not avert,
   This harsh despisal in your eyes I view
      My fainting spirit animates once more.
O gentle cure! O strangest disconcèrt!
   What would one favour do (which ne'er you do)
      When one disfavour doth my life restore?

## LXVI.

*Fermosma do Ceo a nós decida,*
(To Dona Guiomar Henriques?).

Beauty from heavenly heights to Earth descended!
   That leav'st no heart save what thy hest hath bent,
   And satisfying all Intendiment
Without thy being of any thought intended:
What tongue so daring rash that e'er pretended
   Of praising thee pretentious hardiment,
      When every greater gift intelligent,
By thy least value finds its force transcended?

If on thy better part of worth I gaze,
Seeing how opens Earth a heavenly scene,
My genius fails me and my sprite is wrung.
But what more hinders yet to sing thy praise,
Is that when seeing thee I lose my tongue,
And lose my senses when thou be unseen.

## LXVII.

*Poys meus olhos não cansão de chorar*
(Petrarch, "lunga historia").

Since never tire mine eyes to weep alwày
  Griefs never tiring in their trial to tire me ;
  Since ne'er allayed the fire, wherewith to fire me
She hath the power which I could ne'er allay :
Tire not, thou blind-born Love ! to lead astray
  Thither whence never more shall I retire me ;
  Nor cease the world by hearing to inspire me,
Till my weak accents cease to sing my lay.

And if in meads, and dales, and bosky hills
  Ruth linger haply ; haply Love remain
    In birds and beasts ; if sea and stones can feel ;
Hear they the long-drawn history of mine Ills,
  Healed be their pains by witnessing my pain ;
    For only greater sorrows sorrows heal.

## LXVIII.

*Dai-me huma ley, Senhora, de querervos,*
(Written when dismissed the Presence?).

Deal me a Law to love you, Dame ! I pray you,
  So under bail Annoy shall ne'er pursue you,
  For Faith that forces me thus dear to lo'e you,
Eke shall enforce me keep the Law to obey you.
Forbid me all but let these eyne survey you ;
  Let me in spirit-contemplation view you ;
  For an I fail with love-content to endue you,
Leastwise may I with hatred ne'er affray you.

And if this cruel coy Condition
  You deal, to law of Life refuse consent,
    Deal it me, Dame ! albeit law of Death
If e'en you deal not this 'twere well you wone
  Unweeting how my life in grief is spent ;
    Yet will I live content till latest breath.

## LXIX.

*Ferido sem ter cura perecia*
(On being re-admitted?).

A desperate wound was dealt sans hope of heal
  To dure and doughty Telephus, bravest Brave,
  By him a Mother washed in Stygian wave,
And who was harmless from all stroke of steel.
When to Apollo's oracle made appeal
  The Brave, applying how himself to save,
    It answered :—" Wound of self-same weapon crave
Fro' him who wounded and who cure shall deal."

Suchwise my Ladye ! will mine Aventùre
   That I, the sorely wounded by your sight,
Gain from a second sighting Love's recure.
But to my sight so sweet your formosure,
   Here bide I ever like hydropick wight
Whose every draught shall more of drouth assure.


## LXX.

*Na metade do Ceo subido ardia,*
(Echo-Sonnet and first mention of Natercia, *i.e.* Caterina).

Flamed on the midway firmamental hill
   The Shepherd genial-clear, what time 'gan stray
   The Goats from greeny meads, and sought the way
To grateful freshness of a cooly rill :
Under the treën leaves and shadows chill
   The Birds took shelter from the burning ray :
   And, as they ceased their modulated lay,
Naught brake the silence save hoarse chirps of Gryll :

When Shepherd Liso, lone on grass-grown lea,
   Sought where his cruel nymph, Natercia, wonèd
   Wailing with thousands weary sighs his lot ;
" Why flee the lover who fares lost for thee
   To one who loves thee not?" (This wise he
     moanèd) ;
And Echo answered (moaning), *Loves thee not.*

## LXXI.

*Ja e roxa, e branca Aurora destoucava*
(Cf. No. 41).

Now red and white Aurore had loosed the snood
    That snared her delicate golden-huèd hair,
    And bloom-enamelled meadows fresh and fair
Wi' beads of rory Chrystal had bedew'd:
When the two beauteous flocks a-pasture yode
    Commit to Silvio and Laurente's care;
    Swains were the twain and parted was the pair
From one the never-parting Love-god woo'd.

Laurente, weeping truest tears, 'gan cry;—
    "O delicatest Nymph! I ne'er could learn
How one who lives in absence nills to die;
    For life withouten thee as naught I spurn!"
"Love spurns Consenting" (Silvio makes reply),
    "For Death offendeth Esperance of return."

## LXXII.

*Quando de minhas magoas a comprida*
(Of Dinamènè, Petrarch, I. 47).

When of my yearning grief the long offending
    Imagination seals with sleep these eyes,
    She cometh visioned in her Spirit-guise,
Who was in life to me life-dream unending.
There in a Desert-wold, so far extending
    Fails him man's eyèn-sight and fainting dies,
    I fly to reach her; but I feel she flies
Compellèd, faster and still farther wending.

I cry :—" Flee not fro' me, thou Shade benign, ah ! "
She (on me fixing modest glance resign'd
   As one who sayeth, This may never be !")
Flieth again ; and I once more cry " *Dina* " /
But ere the *mènè* come I wake and find
   Even that brief deceit I may not see.


## LXXIII.

*Sospiros inflamados que cantays*
(Conclusion to the Amores ?).


Hot Sighs and Singulfs ! that have voice to sing
   The sorrows making Life a joyous woe ;
   I fare and leave ye, for I fear ye go
Forlore in fording of the Lethe-spring.
Now ye are writ in Script unperishing
   Where all with finger shall your presence show,
   As model-sorrows ; and e'en I allow
That you be sign-posts to the wandering.

In whomso, then, you see large Esperance
   Of Love and Luck (which may to some appear,
Albe misgifts, the happiest ordinance)
   Say him, you served the Pair for many a year,
Say, that in Fortune all is change and chance,
   Say him, that Love is naught but sleight and snare.

## LXXIV.

*Aquella fera humana que enriquece*
(He calls for more suffering and boasts his pains).

That feral Human who her wealth doth owe
　To her presumptuous, prideful surquedry,
　Who robs my vitals, doomed by Love to dree
An Ill that faileth when 'twould greater grow:
If (as it seemeth) Heaven in her would show
　The Show most lovely that the World can see;
　Why make my Life her direst injury?
Why make my Death her vaunt the prowest prow?

Now boast sublime, in fine, your geste victorious,
　Ladye! of taking one so willing tane;
Make my large Story o'er the World memorious:
　The more I see you deal me pang and pain
The more I glory in this gloire so glorious,
　Seeing you glory for-that I be slain.

## LXXV.

*Ditoso seja aquelle que sómente*
(Another cry of Jealousy. Cf. Canz. X. 7).

Happy be mortal man if he lament
　Only disdainful love unkindly coy,
　For coyness never may his hope destroy
Sooner or later to enjoy Content.
Happy be mortal man who Absence-shent
　Can sense no sorrow save remembered joy;
　For albe fear of change may breed Annoy
One feareth Dolour less when sensed by Sent.

Happy, in fine, be any, every plight
  Where love-reserve, deception and disdain
To harm and torture lover's heart delight.
But hapless he who feels repine and blight
  Of wayward error pardon ne'er may gain,
Nor feels the peccant load oppress his sprite.


## LXXVI.

*Quem fosse accompanhando juntamente*
(Written in the Goa prison?   Petrarch, I. 80).


Ah! could I only fare accompanied
  By the true Birdie o'er this greeny plain,
  Who, since her only Mate fro' her was tane,
Knoweth none other joyous time and tide:
And ah! if flying far fro' man I hied,
  With her for neighbour and companion fain,
  She mote assist me to deplore my pain,
And I assist her sore by sorrow tried.

Blest bird! if Nature ne'er for thee endure
Thou to thy firstling add a second fere
She wills thy Sorrows solace shall supply:
But unblest he by long-willed Aventùre
Denièd air enow to breathe a sigh,
And all, in fine, that doth the World ensphere.

## LXXVII.

*O culto divinal se celebrava*
(Petrarch, I. 3.   Comp. Canz. VII. 2).

With holy Worship came they to adore,
  In fane where every creature praised and pray'd,
  The Almighty Maker, who the thing He made
Vouchsafed with holy bloodshed to restore.
There Love, occasion 'biding ever more,
  Where naught of danger my sure Will affray'd,
  With rarest Sprite in Angel-form array'd
My light of Reason like a robber bore.

I (who had deemed the place would lend defence
  And knowing not his customed liberty,
None may escape by over-confidence)
  Yielded me captive, but this day I see,
Ladye! he willed me yours of Will prepense,
  And now repent me I so long was free.

## LXXVIII.

*Leda serenidade deleytosa,*
(To Natercia ?).

A glad delicious air serene that shows
  On Earth-face represented Paradise ;
  Sweet smile 'mid rubies live and pearls of price,
A blush-rose set in gold and virgin snows :
Attunèd presence gracious for repose,
  Where Sense and Daring mingle with advice,
  Teaching how Art conjoining Artifice
Can build up Beauty, e'en as Nature knows :

Accents that either Life or Death engender,
   Rare voice and suave, in fine, my Ladye ! yours ;
     In merriest season Modesty unfeignèd :
These be the weapons make my soul surrender,
   And Love encaptureth me ; but poor his powers
     To rob my glory by surrender gainèd.

## LXXIX.

*Bem sey, Amor, que he certo o que receo ;*
(He encourages Love to deceive him).

Well weet I, Love ! the truth I dread and grieve,
   But thou, to grow thee ever purer pure,
     Denayst it me in perjured sleight secure,
Sworn by thy golden bow—and I believe.
Upon thy bosom I have laid my neave
   Nor see my sorrows through a glass obscure :
     Yet thou'rt so obstinate me to re-assure,
I call me liar, owning I deceive.

Consent not only I by snares be tane,
   I thank thy snaring, and to self deny
Whate'er I see or feel of ban and bane.
   O what strong evil to myself take I !
Who undeceivèd seeing Truth so plain,
   Can still be blinded by a blind-eyed Boy !

## LXXX.

*Como quando do Mar tempestuoso*
(Garcilasso, Sonn. 7).

As when a savèd Waif fro' stormy Main,
  The worn and weary sea-tost sailor-wight
  Swims from the cruel wreck, in woeful plight,
And cannot hear the name of Sea sans pain :
He swears, tho' seeing it a calmy plain,
  It ne'er shall tempt him out of home's delight ;
  Anon, forgetting horrid bygone fright,,
He turns to tempt it, covetous of gain :

Thus I, my Ladye ! 'scaping from the storm
  Stirred by your presence, fly in hope to save me,
    Swearing no similar accident shall find me ;
With spirit alway dwelling on your form
  I turn once more, when greeds of gain embrave me,
    Where erst Misfortune had so nearly tyned me.


## LXXXI.

*Amor he um fogo que arde sem se ver ;*
(Defining Love).

Love is a living Lowe that lurking burneth ;
  'Tis wound that paineth yet ne'er taketh tent ;
  It is one long contented Discontent ;
'Tis Dule which driving mad no Dule discerneth :
Love's Will for nothing save well-willing yearneth ;
  'Tis faring hermit-like in city pent ;
  It is a Malcontent when gained Consent ;
'Tis holding greatest loss most lucre earneth :

It is the being tane with gladdest gree ;
'Tis Winner serving fain the thing he won ;
It is to entreat the slayer loyally.
But how can Love, with all his favour shown,
Cause in our mortal hearts conformity
When Love is love's own foe, most fere of fone ?


## LXXXII.

*Se pena por amarvos se merece,*
(Written for a friend ?).


If Pain the loving-price of you must pay,
  Who shall escape it ?   Who fare fancy-free ?
  What Soul, Sense, Reason, is there that shall see
Your sight, nor instant your behests obey ?
What greater glory can this life array
  Than Thought beguiling with your phantasy ?
  Not sole each rigour, every tormentry
Your sight unpaineth ; nay ! forgot are they.

But an you must destroy them all who loving
  By Love-right only to be yours pretend,
    You will destroy the world which all is yours.
Ladye ! with me you may begin this proving,
  For shows it clearly, and all thoughts intend,
    I love you all I ought with all my powers.

———

*Que levas, cruel Morte?   Hum claro dia.*
(On the death of the Infanta D. Maria, A.D. 1578).

What takest thou, cruel Death ?—"A day all splendid."
  At what hour diddest take 't ?—"At dawn of day."
  Dost thou intend thy prize ?—"Intend it?   Nay!"
Who willed thou take it ?—"HE that it intended."
Who'joys her body?—"Clay-cold Earth that penn'd it."
  How quenchèd was her light ?—"Night o'er it lay."
  What saith our Lusia ?—"She must say her say."
What say ?—"Great Mary my deserts transcended."

Slewst them that saw her ?—"They lay dead before."
  What now saith Love ?—"He durst no word let fall."
  And who doth silence him?—"My will be done."
What to the Court was left ?—"Love-longings sore."
  What there is left to see ?—"No thing at all."
  What glory failed it ?—"Failed this lovely One."

## LXXXIV.

*Ondados fios de ouro reluzente,*
(Memories of an absent Beauty).

Ye wavy wirelets shining golden sheen,
  Now by her lovely hand bound close to head,
  Then o'er her Roses in profusion spread,
You add new graces to the flowery Queen :
Eyes ever softly glancing glance serene,
  With rays divine in burning thousands shed,
  If hence my Soul and Sense are captive led,
Were I but present say what then had been ?

Glad honest laughter, that 'mid finest fine
   Pearl-rows and coral-branch is born to view ;
      Oh, that its honeyed echoes I could hear !
If so much beauty seen with Fancy's eyne
   Make Soul forget herself in gloire so new,
      What when I see her ? Ah ! that I mote see her !

## LXXXV.

*Foy já num tempo doce cousa amar*
(After Natercia's death ?  Petrarch, II. 72).

To love in passèd Time was passing sweet
   While fared I falsèd by one Esperance :
      My heart, high flaming with such furtherance
Melted in Love desire's all-potent heat.
Ah debile Esperance, càduque, fain to fleet !
   How do, in fine, unwheedle Change and Chance !
   For-that the greater Fortune's complaisance,
So much the lesser lasteth her deceit.

Whoso in prosperous gust his lot espied,
   So soon espying the same in bitter pain,
Hath cause to live as though of grief he died.
But whoso trials of this world hath tried,
   Ne grieves ne troubles him the threatened bane :
For customed Evil is an Ill defied.

———

## LXXXVI.

*Dos antiquos Ilustres que deixaraõ*
(Of D. Joam Coutinho).

Of olden Worthies who, by deeds of daring,
   Left names deserving Life o'er Death victorious,
   For light of Time remainèd tales memorious
Of feats the highmost excellence declaring.
An with their actions one attempt comparing
   A thousand feats of yours, each so notorious,
   Your least shall pale their greatest, their most glorious
Done through a many years of life wayfaring.

Theirs was true glory : none their boast shall reave :
As each forth went Fame's several paths to trace
He won his statue in her hero-temple.
You, Portuguezes' and Coutinho's grace,
Noblest Dom John ! a loftier name shall leave
For self a Glut of Gloire, for us Example.

## LXXXVII.

*Conversaçāo domestica afeyçoa,*
(Obscure address, to Belisa?   Cf. Sonn. 91).

Domestick Converse oft shall Love effect,
   Now formed of cleanest Will from error free,
   Then of a loving pity-full quality
Nor one nor other holding in respect.
Then if, peraunter, be your joyaunce checkt
   By sad Unlove and scanty Loyalty,
   Forthright condemneth Truth a False to be
Blind Love, in fine, who pardoneth all Suspect.

Not mere conjecture this I lief assure
  When Thought takes semblance for his evidence,
  To deck man's writ with delicate garniture :
My heave I've placèd on my conscience,
And tell I naught but Truth the purest pure,
  Taught by my tutor, Life's experience.

## LXXXVIII.

*Esforço grande igual ao pensamento,*
(On D. II. de Menezes.  Cf. The Lusiads X. 54).

Strong Force embodying Thought's ideal strain,
   Thoughts proved in action and by deed exprest,
  And ne'er close-lockèd in the craven breast,
To drop, dissolve and die in wind and rain :
Soul that ne'er tempted low-toned greed of gain,
  Digne for this only of what state is best,
  Fere Scourge and sore for ever unreprest
Peoples which haunt the Malabarian Plain :

Grace with rare Beauty corporal allied,
  Adornèd all with pudick continence ;
    Certès high heavenly Work angelick-pure ;
These seld-seen virtues and a more beside,
  Worthy Homerick loftiest eloquence,
    Are laid to lie beneath this sepulture.

_____

## LXXXIX.

*No Mundo quis o tempo que se achasse*
(Written in India? Cf. Sonn. 46 and 48).

Time hath so willèd in the World we find
  Welfare, or certainty or chance begot ;
  And to experiment what bin my lot
Fortune experiment on me design'd.
But that my Destiny impress my mind
  How e'en the hope of Weal became me not,
  Never (so happed) my long-drawn Life-tide wot
One glimpse of things for which I longed and pine'd.

I farèd changing habits, home, estate,
  To see if Change would change a Sort so dure :
  Life to a legier planklet's hand I gave :
But e'en as pleasèd Heaven approve my Fate,
  I've learnt how all my questing Aventùre,
  Hath found that only naught of Luck I have.

## XC.

*A perfeyção, a graça, o doce geito,*
(Very obscure : by D. Manuel de Portugal?).

That Grace most perfect shown by soft sweet Geste,
  That Prime of freshness full, the purest pure,
  In you e'er blooming, for whom Aventùre
Conjoint with Reason conquerèd this breast :
That chrystalline aspect, chastest, modestest,
  In self containing all of Formosure ;
  Those eyes whose splendid lights so softly 'lure,
Whence Love, respecting none, deals strong behest.

An this, in you aye sighted, you would sight,
 As digne from clearest sight to unconceal,
However fancy-free your heart and sprite :
 You'll see the whole its sight to you reveal
Amid this Spirit, where you rule by right,
 That sighting self what feels my Soul you'll feel.


## XCI.

*Vós que de olhos suaves, e serenos,*
(Same argument as Sonn. 87).

You that with suavest orbs of ray serene
 My love to 'prison justest reason show ;
 Condemning every other care and woe
For meaningless, for miserablest mean ;
If jealous Love's domestick draught venene
 You never tasted ; yet I would you know
 How after loving Love shall greater grow,
As of his loving less more cause hath been.

Presume not any there be aught defect,
 Which in the lovèd thing may self present,
Can Love's perfections ever imperfèct :
 Nay Faults but double him and more torment,
For step by step excuse them souls elect
 As Love by contraries hath increment.

## XCII.

*Que poderey do Mundo já querer,*
(On the death of his beloved.   Cf. Sonn. 19).

What expectations from the World have I,
  Since in the lover I so well did will,
  Naught save Disfavour saw I, harmful Ill
And Death, in fine,—what now do more than die?
Since Life of living naught can satisfy,
  Since now I see great Sorrows cannot kill,
  If aught be left of love-grief sadder still
I shall espy it who can all espy.

Death, to my dolour  hath assurance brought
  Of what great Woe be mine ; she is now forlorn
Who erst my soul to feel a fear untaught :
  In Life, 'twas only mine Unlove to mourn ;
In Death, a mighty Dule that haunts my thought.—
  Methinks for this alone my birth was born.

## XCIII.

*Pensamentos, que agora novamente*
(On entering upon a new love).

Fanciful Thoughts ! that now with new intent
  Resuscitate vain Cares whilòm lamented ;
  Say me, ye Thoughts ! still be you not contented
To keep your Keeper in such discontent ?
What Phantasy be this you would present,
  Hour after hour before mine eyes presented ?
  Why with vain dreams attempt heart so prevented
Which nor in dreaming e'er Contentment hent ?

Thoughts ! now I view you wandering from your ways :
   Will not your coyness condescend to say me,
What cunning purpose strays amid this maze ?
   Denay me not, an you would fain denay me ;
For if in wrath ye rise against my days,
   I'll lend you aidance, I myself, to slay me.

## XCIV.

*Se tomo a minha pena em penitencia*
(To his lover whom he had offended).

If by my paining I do penitence,
   Fit punishment for thoughts of kind unkind,
   My woe I soften not, two woes I find ;
Yet this (and more) is preached by Patience ;
And if my deadman's pallid apparence,
   If Sighs and Singulfs scattered vain a-wind,
   Move you not, Ladye ! to more ruth inclined,
Be all mine evils on your conscience.

But an for any asperous chance and change
   Love will all fancy-freest Wills chastise,
     (As in this Evil dooming me I see)
And if (as likely seems) you 'scape revenge,
   Compulsion 'tis (so Love compels his prize)
     I for your sin must pay sin-penalty.

## XCV.

*Aquella que de pura castidade,*
(A classical conceit).

She, who by purest Chastity's decree,
  Wreaked on herself a cruel vengeänce,
  For change so sudden, for so brief a chance,
That smircht her Honour's highest-born degree;
Conquered her beauty was right honestly;
  Conquerèd she, in fine, life's esperance,
  That live immortal so fair sovenance,
Such love, such firmest will, such verity.

Herself, mankind, and all the world forgot,
She smote with dagger dure her downy breast,
In blood the Tyrant's felon violence bathing.
O marvellous Daring! passing strange the Geste!
That giving human clay to Death's short scathing,
Large Life of Memory she should make her lot!

## XCVI.

*Os vestidos Elisa rebolvia,*
(Classical: another conceit).

Oft-times Elisa the dear weed survey'd
  Æneas left her for a pledge memorious;
  The sweet despoilings of a Bygone glorious;
Sweet while her Fortune but assenting aid:
Amid them sighted she the fine-wrought Blade,
  Fit instrument, in fine, for feat notorious;
  And, as a spirit o'er her clay victorious,
So in sad solitary speech she said :—

" Thou new-entempered Blade ! if here remaining
　　Only to execute his fraudful will
　　　(Who did bequeath thee) on my life forlore ;
Know that with me thy fraud is vainest feigning ;
　　For to relieve my life of so much Ill,
　　　The pangs of parting were enough and more.


## XCVII.

*Oh quam caro me custa o intenderte,*
(Cf. Sonn. 91).


Ah me ! how dearly costeth it to trow thee,
　　Molesting Love ! when but thy grace to gain,
　　Fro' Dule thou leadst me Dule-ward to such pain
Where hate and wrath to growth still greater grow thee.
I reckt with knowledge of each phase to know thee,
　　Experience failed me not, nor artful vein ;
　　But now in spirit see I grow amain
The cause that whilom caused me to forego thee.


Thou wast in bosom mine so secret deckt
　　E'en I, who deckt thee, least of all could see
How this concealment did my will subjèct.
　　Now art thou self-discovered ; and so it be
That thy discovery and my own defect
　　This makes me shameful, that injurieth me.

———

## XCVIII.

*Se despoys de esperança taõ perdida,*
(Written in India?).

An after losing Hope so long-lamented,
 Love for some unknown purpose lend assent
 That still some hour I see of short Content
Amid the many this long life tormented ;
For soul so feeble grown, by falling tainted
 (When Fate would raise me to my topmost bent)
 I hold it hopeless Fortune e'er consent
In aught of joyaunce now too late consented.

For Love not only n∧'er my lot hath made
 One hour of life-time spent in joyous gree,
Amid the many to my life denay'd ;
 Nay more, such pain he doth consent I dree,
With my Contentment he fro' me waylaid
 The taste at some one hour Content to see.

## XCIX.

*O rayo cristalino se estendia*
(Follows Sonn. 53. Cf. Virgil, Ecl. 8).

Dispread its sheeny rays in chrystalline weft
 Aurora's marquetry o'er Earth array'd,
 What season Nisè, delicate shepherd-maid,
The home, where left she life, for ever left.
Of eyne, that solar radiänce had reft,
 The light upraising, light with tears bewray'd ;
 By self, by Fortune and by Time betray'd,
Thus cried she, while to Heaven her eyne she heft :

Be born, thou Sol serene, pure-bright of blee ;
   Resplend, thou purple, virgin-white Aurore,
Bringing to saddened Souls new jubilee :
   For mine, I would thou know, that nevermore
In Life contented she thy Sheen shall see
   Nor other Shepherd-maid so woe-forlore.

## C.

*No Mundo poucos annos, e cansados,*
(Epitaph for Péro Moniz?  Cf. Garcil., Sonn. 16).

Few weary Winters in this worldly Pale
   I past, the sport of misery vile and dure :
   So soon my daylight set in night obscure
Of my five lustres saw I not full tale :
O'er lands I marchèd and o'er seas made sail,
   Seeking life's evils or to kill or cure :
But what, in fine, begrudgeth Aventùre
No travails gain us, ban or bane or bale.

Portugal motherèd me : green Alemquer
Was my dear homestead ; but that air pollute
Which ever breathed in this clay-vase of me,
Made me the fishes' food in thee, thou brute
Sea ! lashing Habash, greedy coast and fere,
And ah ! so distant fro' my dear countrè !

# CI.

*Vos que escuitays em Rimas derramado*
(Proëm to Second Century of "Amores": Petrarch, I. 1).

All ye who listen, while my Rhymes proclaim
   The sounds of sighing erst my spirit movèd,
   When through my early youth-tide years I rovèd,
In part another and in part the same :
Know that now only for my Songs I claim
   (What time sang I as Hope or Fear approvèd
   In her whose wrong I felt, her I so lovèd)
Pity not pardon in my care and grame.

Sith well I weet so strong a sentiment
   But made me a by-word in the mouths of men,
      (Which in my self-communion shame I deem)
Serve as clear warning this my chastisement,
   That all the World may ken, and clearly ken,
      What pleaseth mundane Life is briefest Dream.

# CII.

*De Amor escrevo, de Amor trato, e vivo ;*
(By Luis Alvarez Pereira, author of the "Elegiada" ?).

Of Love I write, of Love I treat and live ;
   Love bare my loving which no loving bare ;
   Uncares for everything in life my Care,
Save for what Love's captivity can give.
Love's gift, whose flight fro' high to higher shall strive,
   Basing his glory in that dares he dare ;
   And be depured his dross in rarer air,
Lit by resplendent radiance fugitive.

But ay ! that so much Love gain only Grief,
　More constant Grief as Love is more constant
　　holden,
　For each one only his own triumph wills.
In fine, naught boots me ; for an Hope be lief
　Somewhile a tristful lover to embolden,
　　When near she quickens, when afar she kills.


## CIII.

*Sè da célebre Laura a fermosura*
(Ode VI. 10–11).

An far-famed Laura, beauty's cynosure,
　A Swan of Numbers in his pride extoll'd,
　Thy bard in hand angelick pen must hold,
Since Heaven hath formed thy substance purest pure ;
And if thy Beauty lower-toned Lays allure,
　His praise (Natercia !) were but vainly bold :
　Whilòm to see them Liso's lot was told,
But to describe them fails him Aventùre.

Not Earth but certès Heaven bare thy birth
　Descending here the World with gloire be fraught ;
Who more denies it more his error's worth :
　And thou, I fancy, Earth from Heaven hast sought
To amend the vicious ways contained in Earth,
　With powers divine by thee from Heaven brought.

## CIV.

*Esses cabellos louros, e escolhidos,*
(Another Plaint : written for a friend ?).

These fair-faxt Tresses of the choicest shade,
  Which rob his glories from the golden Sun :
  This airy air immense, which hath undone
My shipwreckt Senses ever more bewray'd :
Those reaving Eyne with sleight of glance array'd,
  Causing my life and death to seem as one,
  This grace divine of tongue, whose every tone
Feigneth my deepest thoughts discredited :

This golden Mean, allied to compast Bearing,
  Doubling of body-gifts the potency ;
Deëss o'er lowly Earth divinely faring !
  Now show they pity, shun they cruelty,
For they be snares Love knits for better snaring,
  In me being sufferance, in you tyranny.

## CV.

*Quem pudèra julgar de vós, Senhora,*
(Complaining of infidelity?   Cf. No. 14).

Whose judgment, Ladye ! could of you discoure
  That Faith so faithful mote to loss pursue you ?
  If I win hatred who for love-boon sue you
I can't unlove you for a single hour.
Would you leave one who dares to love, to adore,
  For one that haply values not to view you ?
  But I am one who ne'er had worth to woo you.
And now I know mine ignorance and deplore.

What wills your Will I ne'er could ascertain,
  Nor of my Will the truth to you could prove,
However seemed such Truth the plainest plain.
  This, while I see you, shall prove perfect tove ;
And, if my loving words persuade in vain,
  I love you more for-that you more unlove.


## CVI.

*Quem, Senhora, presume de louvarvos*
(Of some love-pledge.   Cf. Sonn. 301).

Whoso, my Ladye ! shall presume to praise you
  With speech that shorteth of a speech divine,
  Of so much greater penalty shall be digne,
As grow you greater each time each surveys you.
Aspire no power of Poet-lay to raise you,
  Howe'er seld-found it be or peregrine,
  Such be your charms that Heaven, in fancy mine,
Compare with any save yourself denays you.

Happy this my-your Soul you deign to deem
  Fit to empower with prize of such a cost,        ·
As this you deignèd give in gift supreme :
  This before Life shall take precedence-post ;
Since you have made me Life the less esteem,
  When this for that I'd see right gladly lost.

———

## CVII.

*Moradoras gentis, e delicadas,*
(Garcilasso, Sonn. 11).

Delicate gentle Mays ! who wone where flows
  Glassy and golden Tagus, ye who bide
  Within the grottos where you love to hide,
And 'joy your slumbers sunk in sweet repose.
Now fire your bosom Amor's burning throes
  Within the chrystal Palaces of the tide :
  Then all absorbed you seem in tasks applied
To purfled webs where gold refinèd glows.

Temper the radiance pure of each fair head,
  The light all-lovely of your eyne subdueing,
That floods of sorrow unrestrained they shed.
  So shall you hear with owner grief a-rueing,
Against dour Fortune plaints by me dispread,
  Who plumed with Love-pains fares my steps pur-
    sueing.

## CVIII.

*Brandas aguas do Tejo, que passando*
(Written before going to India?   Cf. Sonn. 158).

Soft Tejo waters ! passing through this Plain
  With irrigated verdure deckt and dight,
  Plants, herbs and flowers, and kine your waves
    delight,
And flow engladdening Nymph and Shepherd-swain :
I know not (ah sweet waters !) know not when
  I shall return to see you ; for such blight,
  Seen how I leave you, deal ye to my sprite,
I go and going despair to come again.

Predestination doomèd unrelenting
 My choicest Blessing turn to weightiest Ill,
  So hard a Parting all mine Ills to double.
For you aye yearning and my lot lamenting,
 With sighs of sorrow other airs I'll fill,
  And other waters with my tears I'll trouble.


## CIX.

*Novos casos de Amor, novos enganos,*
(Experientia docet. Cf. Sonn. 93 and 98).


New change and chance of Love, new snare and sleight
 Enwrapt in glozing flatteries well-known;
  False promises of weals that hidden wone,
Whose lurking evils open damage dight!
How take ye not to undeceive your sight,
 So many a wasted tear so many a moan,
  For ne one life ne thousand lives should own
So many a day, so many a year of night?


Now a new mister heart exchange I must,
 And other eyne unwont to be your prey,
Again to trust you as I once could trust.
 Ye Snares! with me ensnarèd wend your way,
And some day think ye, an to think ye lust,
 What of the sorely knived men wont to say.

---

## CX.

*Onde porey meus olhos que não veja*
(Cf. Sonn. 48 and Canz. 9).

Where shall I bend these eyne that be unseen
  The cause which bare what Ills my heart torment?
  What part shall fare I with a Thought intent
On Rest imparted to my restless teen?
How snarèd he who longs (now well I ween)
  In Amor's vanities for true Content
  When in his gusts which are but windy vent
Weal ever fails and Ill grows keener keen.

And more, on Disillusion made full clear,
  This subjugated Soul so quells my Thought
    That on Illusion hangeth my Desire;
And yede I day by day, and year by year,
  Chasing a What-is-it, chasing a Naught
    Which seemeth lesser as I draw me nigher.

## CXI.

*Já do Mondego as aguas aparecem*
(He takes leave of the Coimbran. Cf. Sonn. 133).

Now of Mondego-stream the waters show
  Unto mine eyes, not mine but alien eyes,
  Which, full of waters welling otherwise,
Seeing the pleasant vision fuller grow.
Meseems the Waters eke enforcèd flow,
  E'en as detained by mazy turns and ties.
  Woe's me! How many a mode, how many a guise
Hath after-pyne to breed me sadder Woe!

A life so many Ills have plunderèd
   Love in such terms hath placed, by doubt I'm tost
An to this Journey's end it shall be sped.
   Nay more, Life holdeth self as wholly lost,
Seeing by Soul 'tis unaccompanièd;
   That lingers still when Life gave up the ghost.


## CXII.

*Que doudo pensamento he o que sigo?*
(By the Conde de Vimioso? Cf. Sonn. 92).


What be this madding Thought I nill forego?
   Why fare I following vain-visioned end?
   Ah woe is me! who cannot self intend;
Nor what I say nor what unsay can know.
I war with one who cometh peace to show;
   'Gainst one who wars me self I can't defend:
   Fro' so false esperance what can I pretend?
Who makes me friendly with the woes I owe?

Why, an free-willèd born, myself enslave?
And if I will it, wherefore will it not?
How with unsnaring am I snared so lief?
Why hope, if hopeless erst, for hopeful lot?
And why not live if still some Hope I have?
And if I live why gird at deadly grief?

## CXIII.

*Hum firme coraçaõ posto em ventura,*
(To Violante? Cf. No. 119).

A constant heart by hazard made unsure ;
　　An honest longing that would fain reject
　　Your crude conditions, which in naught respect
My love so purely pure, my faith so pure :
A viewing you to ruth's kind use and ure
　　Eternal enemy, garreth me suspect
　　Some fere Hyrcanian did your lips allect,
Or you were born the birth of rock-womb dure.

I fare me seeking Cause, that shall explain
　　So strange a Cruelty, yet the more I do,
　　　The more I labour, more it treats me ill.
Hence comes it no one but condemns us twain ;
　　You who would kill the love which loves you so ;
　　Me for so loving one whose cruelties kill.

## CXIV.

*Ar, que de meus suspiros vejo cheyo ;*
(How he loves against Nature's order).

Air ! I see chargèd with my heavy sighs ;
　　Earth ! tired e'en now my torment to maintain ;
　　Water ! which thousands of my tears sustain ;
Fire ! I make fiercer in my breast arise :
At peace in me you meet ; thus I devise,
　　Though ye so fair intent may never deign ;
　　For where in dolours there is dearth of pain,
Life is sustainèd by your energies.

Ay hostile Fortune! ay vindicative
  Amor! to what discourse for you I fare,
    Yet may not move you by my sorrow's worth!
If ye would kill me wherefore do I live?
  How am I living, I that have contràyr
    Fire, Fortune, Amor, Water, Air and Earth?


## CXV.

*Já claro vejo bem, já bem conheço*
(Another Plaint).

Now ken I clearly, clearly I believe
  How ever add I caring to my Care,
    That I on water build and write on air,
And seely Cosset from the Wolf I'd reave;
That I'm Arachne who with Pallas weave;
    That to the Tyger wail I my despair;
    That in small pipkin squeeze the Seas I dare,
When I (unworthy) would this Heaven achieve.

Peace I would conquer 'mid a hubble infernal;
  By night Sol's aureate beams I seek to see;
And tepid Prime-tide in the Cold hybernal:
  I seek in bright Olympus blackest blee;
And wisht-for welfare in mine Ills eternal
  When I seek love-grace of your cruelty.

———

## CXVI.

*De cà, donde somente o imaginarvos*
(By some attributed to F. R. L. Surrupita).

Hence (where to image you and only you
   This rigorous Absence doth my thought constrain)
   Borne upon Love-wings plied with daring strain,
Seeks you my Soul that ill her Ills doth rue :
And feared she not to fire you with the lowe,
   The burning flames your cause doth aye maintain,
   There would she wone and, to your presence tane,
How to content you from yourself would know.

But as her Absence is parforce design'd,
   You as her Ladye hence she acknowledgeth,
Over your idol'd feet a slave incline'd ;
   And sith you see her purely profferèd faith,
Thence turn those glances on her cares unkind,—
   More you must give her than she meriteth.

## CXVII.

*Naõ ha louvor que arribe a menor parte*
(Cf. Sonn. 17, 103, and 106).

There be no praises reach the minim part
   Of what, fair Ladye ! in your form we view ;
   You are your praises : who adoreth you
To this (naught else) reduceth wits and art.
What gifts to many Nature would repart
   Of fair and fetis, so in you congrue
   Suchwise conjoinèd, it were due and true
To say the Members they and you the Heart :

Then 'tis no fault o' mine if, daring praise you,
    I see all praises impotently end,
Since Heaven o'er earthly things so high would raise
    you :
    Yea, be the fault your charms that so resplend ;
And I their fault forgive, and give to appraise you
    So lofty praises every praise transcend.


## CXVIII.

*Naõ vds ao Monte Nise, com teu gado,*
(From the Spanish. Cf. Sonn. No. 120).

Lead not thy lambkins, Nisè, to yon crest
    Where I saw Cupid in thy search persèver,
    For thee alone all comers asking ever
Rather with angry mien than placid geste.
Abroad he bruits, in fine, thou stolst his best
    Of bolts and arrows storèd in his quiver ;
    And sware so ardent dart he would deliver
That shall pass through and through that delicate
    breast.

Fly far from seeing such misaventùre,
    For an thou hold he have for thee a spite,
Haply he reach thee with his hand-grasp dure.
    But ay ! how vainly counsels thee my fright,
If to thine ever peerless formosure
    His mightiest dart surrender all its might !

———

## CXIX.

*A Violeta maes bella que amanhece*
(To Violante. Cf. Sonn. 13).

The daintiest Violet which a-morning blown
    Amells the valley dight in garb of green,
    With her pale lustre and her modest mien,
Thee, Violante, Beauty's Queen must own :
Dost ask me why ?   Because in thee alone
    Her name and purer tints and hues are seen ;
    And she must study from thy brow what mean
The highest powers by bloom of beauty shown.

O lustrous floret ! O Sol fairest fair !
    Sole robber of my senses ! pray thee *I* do
Allow not Love of loving be so spare.
    O thou transpiercing arrow of Cupìdo !
What wouldst thou ?  In this valley for repayre
    Prithee I play Æneas to this Dido.


## CXX.

*Tornay essa brancura á alva açuçena,*
(From the Spanish ?).

Give back this blanchness to the Lily's skin,
    To purpling Rose these blushes purely bright :
    Give back to Sol the flame of living light
Shown by this face that shows the robber's sin.
Give back to dulcet-voicèd Melusine
    The voice whose cadence is a mere delight :
    Give back the Graces' grace who all unite
To 'plain you made their lustre less serene.

Give back to lovely Venus loveliness ;
   Give back Minerva's genius, lore and art,
      And chaste cold Dian's chastest purest blee :
Come, doff these borrowed plumes, this goodliness
   Of gifts, and you shall wone in every part
      Sole with yourself, which is sole Cruelty.


## CXXI.

*De mil suspeitas vans se me levantað*
(By Diogo Bernardes ?   Cf. Sonn. 70).


Fro' vain suspicions in a thousand ways
   Rise disappointments, griefs veridical.
      Ah ! that the charm of Love be magick all
That with I wot-not-what my soul waylays !
As Sirens, softly sing their sugrèd lays,
   Sea-faring men with fatal snare to thrall ;
      So lure me on my songs phantastical
And eft with thousand horrid thoughts amaze.

When fain I fancy port or land to take,
   Sudden so stormy rage of wind ariseth,
      At once for Life I fear and disconfide.
Yet on myself the fiercest war I make,
   Since, known what risks for lovers Love deviseth,
      Self-trusting still I trust to Love's own tide.

## CXXII.

*Mil vezes determino naõ vos ver*
(Imitated from his " Ennius," Bernardim Ribeiro).

I swear a thousand times to unsee your sight,
   And see if Absence soothe a heart distraught ;
   And if I think of pain to self so wrought,
Think what 'twould be an 'twere to me bedight.
Imports me little now more suffering plight,
   Since Love to such a point my case hath brought ;
   Yet what most grieves me is the grievous thought
Ill could I live without this undelight.

Thus seek I nowise Cure to heal my Care,
   For were I seeking Cure, right well I wot
     In this same point my loss would prove complete.
Would you so rigorous life, in fine, I bear ?
   Only your love-boon can convene my lot.
     Is it your will that so it be ?  So be it !

## CXXIII.

*A chaga que, Senhora, me fizestes,*
(To a nun of the order Das Chagas ?  Cf. Sonn. 77).

The wound, Senhora ! you have doomed me dree
   Was not a hurt to heal in single day ;
   Nay, it increaseth in so crescive way,
That proves intention in your cruelty.
Causing such grief were you of grieving free ?
   But to your grieving grief I would denay,
   Sith to my sight it would some hope convey
Of what you willèd ne'er be seen in me.

Those Eyne, whose puissance me of me bereft,
    Causèd this evil e'er I undergo ;
Yet fare you feigning you ne'er caused the theft :
    But I'll revenge myself! And when d' you know ?
Whenas I see you 'plaining that you left
    My soul go burning in their living lowe.

## CXXIV.

*Se com desprezos, Ninfa, te parece*
(He vaunts his constancy).

An thy despisal, Nymph ! thou haply trow
    Can ever deviate from its course of Care
A Heart so constant, which hath vowed a vow
    In bearing torment highest boast to bear :
Doff thy persistency, and learn to know
    Illy thou knowest Love grown wise and ware ;
For knowst and kennest not thy Wrongs make grow
    My growth of Ills as more unloved I fare.

The coy Unlove thou doomest me essay,
Convert to pity, an be not thy will
With thine Unwill my love still higher stye.
Ne'er hope to conquer me by cruellest Ill :
Well canst thou slay me and well dost thou slay,
But my Presumption's life shall never die.

———

*Senhora minha, se eu de vós ausente*

(Garcilasso, No. 9 : a mere translation).

Senhora mine ! driven self fro' you to absent
   If I could parry thrust of pain so rare,
   Suspect I 'twould offend the love I bear,
Forgetting welfare by your presence lent :
Further, now feel I other accident,
    And 'tis that seeing if I of life despair,
    I lose the boast and hope of seeing my Faire,
With only difference in my detriment :

And in such difference all my senses biding
    Fight one another with so fierce outrànce,
    I judge mine Ills inhuman, unhumane.
I see division sense from sense dividing ;
    And if concording any day, perchance,
    'Tis but in plotting for my better bane.


## CXXVI.

*No regaço da May Amor estava*

(On a picture of Venus and Child).

Lapt by his Mother little Love was lying,
   So lovely sleeping that the sight could wrest
   Freedom from every fancy-freest breast,
And his own Mother near-hand do to dying.
She sat with curious eye his form espying
    Which hath so direly all the world opprest ;
    When soft he murmured in a dream's unrest
"She caused all Evils all are now abying."

Soliso, graduate in the school of Love,
   Who best to know the two had aventùre
Thus did the Shepherds' doubt and dread remove :
   " An hurt and harm my heart withouten cure
The Son, whose red-hot shafts my bosom rove,
   The Mother's beauty harmeth more forsure."


## CXXVII.

*Esse terreste Cáos com seus vapores*
(Much admired.  Cf. " The Lusiads," X. 6).


This earthly Chaos, with its vaporous layer,
   May ne'er condense to base contagious cloud,
   But that clear Sol shall rend the racking shroud
With his own lucent radiance rarely fair :
This coy ingratitude, this rigorous air,
   Are the foul ugly mists that fronting crowd,
   Till Heaven convert to weeping long and loud
Its vain fond esperance and its favours spare.

Earth may to Heaven her rondure interpose :
   Eclipse for hours the sight of Sol may hide ;
   But ne'er endureth light convert to shade :
Haply your warfare shall o'ercome its foes ;
   But maugre every cloud, clear, purified
   Shall shine your Sun by all mankind obey'd.

———

## CXXVIII.

*Huma admiravel erva se conhece,*
(He is like a certain Indian herb).

In Hind an admirable herb is known,
   That fares from hour to hour the sun enfacing
   When forth he comes from Euphrat-bank upracing,
And when he's zenith'd then it blooms full-blown.
But, as his charet welks a-sea to wone,
   Then Flora forfeits charms the most engracing,
   For wanness wilts her pride, all hues effacing:
So loss of sunlight gars her woe-begone.

My Sun ! whene'er you gladden my-your sprite,
Showing the favour very life bestows,
You bring luxuriant bloom my Soul contenting :
But soon unseeing you and whelmed in woes,
She wilts and withers with her fierce tormenting
Nor is there any bears your absence-blight.

## CXXIX.

*Creccy, desejo meu, poys que a Ventura*
(His loving hopes of a happy end. Cf. Sonn. 31).

Grow ye my Longings ! sithence Aventùre
   You in her arms vouchsafed to raise and rear ;
   For the fair Cause that such a birth could bear
The happiest ending doth for you ensure.
If bold aspirings to such height allure,
   Fear not so near-hand unto Sol to fare ;
   Likest the Royal Erne's be now your care,
Who proves him purer more he doth endure.

Take heart, my heart ! the very Thought has lent
 A power to gar thee grow more glorious-great,
Without regarding aught thy meritment.
 Thou must grow stronger still by force innate ;
For an of bravery born was thy Intent,
 Now doth its Daring make it fortunate.

## CXXX.

*He o gozado bem em agua escrito ;*
(Metaphysico-amorous.   Cf. Sonn. 31 and 229).

Weal, once enjoyèd, is on water writ ;
 Love wones in longing, dies he in the effect :
 Only can Longing longed-for Gifts perfect,
Sith it has something of the Infinite.
To gift with Goods prescribed the immortal Sprite
 In purest-perfect Love, were mere defect :
 By mode superior, failures ne'er affect,
You I except from limits here indite.

By force of Esperance evermore unknown,
 By faith of man's desire and man's despair,
More of desire you'll win when you are won.
 You can't be loved for Esperance bald and bare :
Loved you shall be when seen, believed when shown ;
 But not sans injury dare we try Compare.

## CXXXI.

*De quantos gracas tinha a Natureza.*
(To an Angelica? Cf. Sonn. 137).

Nature of all her graces infinite
　Formèd a Treasury filled with rarest show ;
　And with her Rubins, Roses, Gold and Snow,
Framèd that form sublime, Angelick-bright.
Rubins in lips she set, on the pure light
　Of face I die for, garred she Roses grow ;
　Taught the blonde metal in the locks to flow,
And snowed the bosom that enfires my sprite.

But in those eyne her Power showed best display ;
　She made of them a Sun that doth depure
Radiance to clearer than the clearest day.
　For brief, my Ladye, in your ornature
She lavisht purity (far as Nature may)
　Of Rubins, Roses, Snow, bright Gold, Light pure.


## CXXXII.

*Nunca em Amor damnou o atrevimento ;*
(Audaces Fortuna juvat : Be Bold : De l'audace, &c.).

Love ne'er condemnèd hearts that boldly dare ;
　Fortune aye favoured man's audacity ;
　For ever weighteth shrinking Cowardry,
Like stone, man's Thought which should be free as air.
Who to sublimest Firmament would fare
　His guide and Lode-star there alone shall see ;
　For Weal enhearsèd in man's phantasy
Is but illusion fit for breeze to bear.

We fain must open paths for Aventùre :
  None save by proper self to Fortune rose ;
  And Fate doth only first beginnings breed.
To dare is Valour, not fool's use and ure.
  The heart of craven all its chance shall lose
  If, seeing you, it may not Fear unheed.


## CXXXIII.

*Doces, e claras aguas do Mondego,*
(Adieu to Coimbra.  Cf. Sonn. 212 : Elegy I.).

Sweet lucent waters of Mondego-stream,
  Of my Remembrance restful jouïssance,
  Where far-fet, lingering, traitorous Esperance
Long whiles misled me in a blinding Dream :
Fro' you I part, yea, still I'll ne'er misdeem
  That long-drawn Memories which your charms
      enhance
  Forbid me changing and, in every chance,
E'en as I farther speed I nearer seem.

Well may my Fortunes hale this instrument
  Of Soul o'er new strange regions wide and side,
Offered to winds and watery element :
  But hence my Spirit, by you 'companied,
Borne on the nimble wings that Reverie lent
  Flies home and bathes her, Waters ! in your tide.

---

## CXXXIV.

*Senhor Joaõ Lopez, o meu baxo estado*
(About some light o' love.   Cf. Sonn. 62).

Sir John Lopèz! yestreen my low estate
  I saw upraised to rank so excellent,
  E'en you, by all men envièd, would consent,
For my Fate only to exchange your Fate.
I saw the geste so suave, so delicate,
  That dealt you erst Content and Discontent,
  I heard the gentle voice to winds outsent,
Serening air and soothing bane and bate.

I saw her saying as much in words as few
As none in many; but myself I find
Dying but to hear those honeyed accents flow.
Ah! woe worth Fortune and the Boy born blind,
Him, for obliging hearts such Ills to rue;
Her, who unequal lots doth still bestow.

## CXXXV.

*A Morte que da vida o nó desata*
(Cupio dissolvi, &c.).

Death, who our life-knot loveth to unknit,
  The knots Love knitted would asunder shear
  With Absence, sword-blade keen o'erhanging near,
And Time abetting who doth all unfit:
Two foes that each would slay his opposite,
  Death against Love conjoins in union fere;
  This, Reason warring Fortune's will austere;
That, thankless Fortune Reason fain to outwit.

But prove his potent, high, imperial Power
Death, when fro' body he departs the sprite,
Love in one body twinnèd souls shall mate;
That bear the Palm-wreath with triumphant might .
Fro' Mors strong Amor, 'spite of Absence-stowre,
And Power of Time, of Reason and of Fate.


## CXXXVI.

*Arvore, cujo pomo bello, e brando,*
(To a Rose-apple tree under which sat his lover).


Tree! on whose gracious Pome we see the trace
   Of blood and milk by Nature's art depinct;
   Upon whose cheek the rosy snowy tinct
Rivals the radiance of the virginal face.
Ne'er with the wuthering winds, whose raging race
   Uproots the tree-bole, may thy lot be linkt;
   Nor airy malice view in thee extinct
The varied colours now thy fruitage grace;

And eke thou showerest suave and suitable shade
On my Contentment, while thy perfumed scent
Flavours the glory that be-favours me;
And if my merit fail thy meritment
Singing thy praises, leastways be thou made
'Gainst days of sorrow one sweet Memory.

----

## CXXXVII.

*O filho de Latona esclarecido,*
(Petrarch, Triumph of Love, end of Chap. I.).

Latona's son, by clearest light belit,
  Who gladdeth mortals with his genial ray,
  Prevailed the Worm Pythonickal to slay
Whose bite slew thousands ere the biter bit.
He smote with bow and eke with bow was smit,
  Whose golden arrows clove their glowing way,
  Where meads Thessalian softly smiling lay,
And the Peneian Nymph was she that hit.

Nothing availèd him to cure his pain,
  Wisdom, respect, ne diligent watch and ward,
For all his being celestial, sovereign:
If then a god unsaw the snaring bane
  Of one so humble-mean in his regard,
What hope from Maid of more than mortal main?

## CXXXVIII.

*Presença bella, Angelica figura,*
(To an Angelica? Cf. Sonn. 131).

Beautiful presence, form of Angel-grace,
  Where Heaven's choicest Heaven made our own;
  Glad geste in garden where the Rose is sown,
'Mid Roses smiling with a rosier face.
Eyne in whose depths such minglement we trace
  Of chrystal marquetry'd with onyx-stone,
  For orbs of delicate green have ever shown
Not greenth of Hope but Envy obscure base.

Grace, Softness, Prudence, gifties e'er increasing
The natural Beauties with an honest Scorn,
(Whereby the scornèd Charms more honour win)
Like prisons hold a heart, which prisoner borne,
Singeth to clanking chains its pains so pleasing,
As sings the Siren o'er the stormy din.

## CXXXIX.

*Por cima destas aguas forte, e firme,*
(Written en route to Goa?   Cf. Sonn. 24 and 35).

Wi' firm and forceful heart ferforth I'll hie
   Over these waves where'er Fate orderèd,
   Since o'er the briny floods I saw beshed
By those clear eyne, I found the force to fly.
The parting-season now had passèd by ;
   Now 'spite a thousand stumbling blocks I sped,
   Where all Love's torrent-streams were traversèd
That would to parting steps a pass deny.

I passed the Passes with that pushing pride,
   Wherewith a glorious Death and certain Fate
The conquered mortal unto Wanhope guide.
In what new figure, in what form untried
   Shall come to daunt and frighten Death irate
One at Death's feet surrenderèd and tied ?

## CXL.

*Tal mostra de si dà vossa figura*
(To an Isabel ?   Written for a friend ?).

So doth your semblance show to 'raptured viewer
   Sibela ! globèd Earth's resplendent light,
   That forceful Nature and creative might
Glow with your purer presence kindlier pure.
What man hath seen sure conquest so secure,
   So singular enamel beauteous-bright,
   Who shall not suffer ills of iller plight,
If he attempt resist such lovely lure ?

I, then, to excuse and 'scape disdain so coy,
Before my Thought made Reason bow and bend,
And saw my Senses soon his captives tane.
But an my Daring you perchance offend,
A novel vengeance you may yet enjoy
On the life remnants that to me remain.

## CXLI.

*Na desesperação já repousava*
(He consoles himself with the pleasures of Despair).

In Desperation 'gan repose espy
   My bosom's Lord, so long, so deeply painèd ;
   And (concert with eternal loss attainèd)
I dreaded nothing, naught of hope had I :
When a vain shadow lured me to rely
   On some fair boon for me mote be ordainèd
   In formous form whose counterfeit remainèd
Ensoul'd, and raised me unto height so high.

What ready credit hearts have ever lent
  To that they covet with a fixèd will,
    If once their hard-heart Destiny they forget !
Ah ! Leave me error : I am heart-content ;
  For though my lesser grow to greater Ill,
    Remain the glories Fancy doth beget.


## CXLII.

*Diversos dões reparte o Ceo benino,*
(Cf. Sonns. 44 and 120).


Distribute sundry boons the Heavens benign,
  Willing each spirit own but single boon;
    Thiswise with chastest bosom He deckt the Moon
Who lights the primal sphere, the chrystalline :
Grace made the Mother of the Boy to shine.
  Who in this vision feels her charms outshone ;
    Pallas had learning ne'er excelled thine own,
And fell to Juno noble empire digne.

But now large Heaven deigns on thee outpour
  The most He owneth, and 'twere but a trace,
    Respecting whatso Nature's Author be.
Lend thee, fair Dame ! unlief to lend their store
  Luna chaste bosom, Venus all her grace,
    Her learning Pallas, Juno empery.

———

## CXLIII.

*Gentil Senhora, se a Fortuna imiga*
(Written en route to Ceuta?).

If, Ladye fair ! my Fortune, ferest foe,
  Who against my welfare plots with all the skies,
  Debar these eyne from dwelling on those eyes,
That she pursue me with a sorer blow ;
I bear this spirit bound to undergo
  Wrath's direst pressure, fire, sea-injuries,
  Vowing you Memory that for ever sighs
Only with you unending lien to owe.

In this my Sprite where Fortune fails of force,
  So live I'll keep you, famine, frost and flame
    Shall ne'er out-drive you, ne most parlous plight.
Rather, with accents tremulous and hoarse
  Calling on you, and only in your name
    The winds and all my foes I'll force to flight.

## CXLIV.

*Que modo taõ sutil da Natureza*
(To one taking the Fanciscan veil in 1572).

What novel show of Nature's subtleties
  The World and every worldly snare to fly,
  Allows thee hide, ere thy green years go by,
So fresh young beauties 'neath a frock of frieze !
Yet can it never hide that high-bred ease,
  The gracious gravity of that sovran eye,
  Before whose radiance 'mid the lave have I
Lost all resistance, lost all energies.

Whoso would fare him free of griefs and pains,
   Seeing and bearing her in thought memorious,
By very self of Reason self condemns.
   For who deservèd sight of charms so glorious
Must live a prisonèd wight ; since Love ordains
   In her own right She claim to be victorious.


## CXLV.

*Quando se vir com agoa o fogo arder,*
(On an attempt to remove his lover).


When man sees water burn with blazing lowe
   And brightest Dayshine mate with blackest Night ;
   When Earth upheaves her depths to highmost height,
Where Heaven his own prerogative doth show :
   When Love at Reason's feet shall lout him low
   And Fortune level all with equal right,
   I will forego to see that fairest sight
And then, the sight foregone, Love I'll unknow.

But since hath never seen such change, such chance,
   The World, for-that, in fine, no sight e'er sees it,
   None seek to wean me fro' my love of you,
Basta, that bide in you mine Esperance
   To save my Soul or, an you please, to leese it,
   Ne'er shall mine eyes consent your sight to unview.

---

## CXLVI.

*Quando a suprema dor muito me aperta,*
(His greatest misery would be to forget).

When I (by sùpreme miseries opprest)
  Say 'tis my wish forgetfulness to find,
  'Tis but a violence offered to my mind,
And nills Free-will obey such tyrant-hest.
Then rouseth me from fault the faultiest
  Light in a saner intellect enshrine'd,
  Showing 'tis foolish thought or feigning kind
To say such resting bringeth certain rest.

For this true Image, which hath represented
  In mind the single Good I must forego,
After a fashion shows my hand hath hent it.
  Then blest and blissful grows the Grief I owe,
Sith by its causing I enjoy contented
  A Weal that e'en unseeing you I know.


## CXLVII.

*Na margem de hum ribeyro, que fendia*
(Natercia married?).

On bank of brooklet, cleaving with its tide
  Of liquid chrystalline, a fair green plain,
  Sombre with sorrow Liso (hapless swain)
On bole of mountain-ash enpropt thus cried :—
" Cruel Natercia ! Who doth so misguide
  Thy kindly caring for my care-full bane?
  If undeceivèd I must dree such pain,
By thee deceivèd ever mote I bide."

What of that faith and troth to me thou plightedst?
What of that purest love that showed its fairest?
Who could so readily do all undone?
When with those Eyne another's love thou sightedst,
How couldst forget what oath to me thou swarest
By all their splendours, thou wast mine, mine own?"

## CXLVIII.

*Se me vem tanta gloria só de olharte,*
(Sufistical : Love's loss is his gain).

If I so triumph but because I view thee,
I see more sorrow when mine eyes unsight thee :
If I would merit thee by praise I write thee,
Largely I pay false hopes to woo and sue thee.
If as thou be my praise aspire to approve thee,
I know that I as I shall but despight thee,
If ill I will myself for Will I plight thee,
What more can will or wish I save to love thee?

How aids me not this love of rarest guise?
O human treasure ! O sweet blessing glorious !
Happy the man who deathward for thee hies !
Writ in my thoughts thy name shall last memorious ;
This soul shall live because for thee she dies ;
Since battle's issue is to be victorious.

## CXLIX.

*Sempre a Razão vencida foy de Amor.*
(Cf. Sonn. 36, 46, and 49 : Canz., VII. 5 : Ecl. II. 27.)

By Amor routed Reason aye hath been ;
   But when my heart with pleading 'gan assail,
   Love granted power of Reason to prevail,
Now what more curious case has man e'er seen !
New mode of dying, new griefs evergreen !
   A mighty marvel ! admirable tale !
   That Love of vigour at the end should fail,
Lest of its vigour fail Love's vigorous teen.

Never was frailty in true loving known ;
   Nay, this wise ever gaineth more of might
One foe that other foe would see o'erthrown.
   But Reason who, in fine, can win such fight
I hold not Reason ; liefer would I own
   'Tis inclination to my own despight.

## CL.

*Coytado, que em hum tempo choro, e rio ;*
(Cf. Sonn. 9).

Poor I ! who laugh and cry at single tide ;
   Feel Hope and Wanhope, love and yet abhor ;
   Conjointly Life enjoy, and Life deplore ;
And in one thing confiding disconfide.
Wingless I fly, withouten eyes I guide ;
   Of what I merit most I hold least store ;
   Then speak I better when of speech forlore ;
Uncontradicted all I override.

For me the Impossible makes all possible ;
 By Change I struggle gain of rest to get ;
  To be a captive, to be free as air :
I would be seen, I would be invisible ;
 Would 'scape the netting and yet love the net ;
  Such are the extremes wherein this day I fare !


## CLI.

*Julgame a gente toda por perdido,*
("The world well lost ").


The world misjudgeth I have lost my lot,
 Seeing me lover-like so 'joy my pain,
  So shun my neighbours, far fro' man remain,
Forgetting human commerce and forgot :
But as all knowledge of the world I wot,
 And view its doublings from a higher plane,
  I hold him rustick, cozened, base of strain,
Who with my Love-grief greater groweth not.

Revolve, revolving aye, Earth, Main and Wind ;
 At wealth and honours let the vulgar fly,
  Oe'rcoming fire and steel and heat and cold.
Let me in Love alone Contentment find,
 Ensculpturèd thro' timeless Time to espy
  Your lovely semblance in my soul ensoul'd.

## CLII.

*Olhos, aonde o Ceo com luz maes pura,*
(Cf. Sonn. 38).

Eyes ! wherein heavenly radiance purest pure
   Willed of His puissance show most certain sign,
   An ye would rightly see how strong you shine,
View me the Creature of your self, the Viewer !
In me you'll view your living portraiture,
   Properer than shrined in purest Chrystalline,
   Because you'll certès view in Soul of mine,
Clearer than Chrystalline, your formosure.

For mine I only wish my Wish to see,
   If more for loving haply be my due,
      That mote your powers enseal me for your thrall.
I see no worldly memory in me :
   All I forget remembering you, and you
      O'er me triumphant I o'ertriumph all.

## CLIII.

*Criou a Natureza Damas bellas,*
(How excellent is his lover : written for a friend ?).

Nature bare lovely Dames, and Poet's lay
   Wi' deathless lyre-quills in their laud delighted ;
   Their parts most prizèd she in you united,
And all their bestest made you, Dame ! display.
They in your presence show the Star's pale ray
   And, seeing you, starken in eclipse benighted ;
   But an they have for Sun those rosy-lighted
Rays of more radiant Sun, thrice happy they !

In grace, perfection and in gentle rede,
  By mode to mortals certès peregrine,
This Beauty all things beauteous doth exceed.
  O could I borrow part of the Divine
To merit you ! but if pure Love you heed
  As aught availing, I of you am digne.


## CLIV.

*Que esperays, Esperança ? Desespero.*
(Dialogue : he will love against hope.)

Hope ! what of hoping own you ?—"I despair."
  What, then, hath Wanhope caused?—"A variance."
  You, Life, how fare you ?—"Lorn of esperance."
What say you, Heart?—"In fondest love I fare."
What, Soul, feel you ?—"That Love brings cruel care."
  In fine, how live you ?—"Sans a hope in chance."
  What, then, sustaineth you ?—"One sovenance."
Is this your only hope ?—"Hope's sole repair."

Where can you take your stead ?—"Here where I
      wone."
  And where now wone you ?—"Where my life is
      dead."
    And hold you Death a weal ?—"Love wills so
      be."
Who dooms you thus ?—"Myself to self beknown."
  Who may you be ?—"One self surrenderèd."
    To whom surrender'd ?—"To one dearest she."

## CLV.

*Se como em tudo o maes fostes perfeyta,*
(Her cruelty and his resignation : for a friend ?).

If, as in all things else you be perfècted,
  Your coy condition were less fugitive,
  Then would my Fortune at high goal arrive,
Then would its height to you be more subjècted.
But when my life is at your feet dejected,
  And you accept not, Life-tide nills survive :
  Life of herself would me of me deprive, ⚫
Rejecting me because by you rejected.

An Life in loving you your Will oppose,
  Command, my Ladye ! that she end mine ills
    And the profoundest sadness e'er I dree :
Yet she refuses me, not that she knows
  A touch of pity, but on me she wills
    To grant you glutting of your cruelty.

## CLVI.

*Se algum' hora essa vista maes suave*
(Written for a friend ?).

If your douce Vision at some hour you deign
  Haply to grant me, ere one moment went
  I feel such joyaunce, sense so full Content,
Fear I no losses, dread ne ban ne bane.
But when with scorn so sore, so dour disdain
  That beauteous face whole-hearted you present,
  I prove such torment, pangs so vehement,
Tis mighty marvel life survives the pain.

So doth my life-tide or the death of me
  Hang from an eye-glance; your prerogative
    Dealeth me life or death with glance of eye.
Happy if grant me Heaven or Destiny
  You give me life that back to you I give,
    Or death because I only crave to die!


## CLVII.

*Tanto se forað, Ninfa, costumando*
(For a friend?).


So farèd, Nymph! self-customing these Eyne
 To weep what sorrows dealt thy Will so dure,
 That now they thole, by Nature's use and ure,
What sufferings Accident did first assign.
Hours due to sleeping I in waking pine
  And watch, of nothing sauf of sorrow sure:
  But all my weepings ne'er thy harshness cure
Though ever weep and weep these eyes of mine.


This wise from woe to woe, from grief to grief,
  They wear themselves away in vain, in vain,
    And eke my hapless life they wear away.
To water Love-fire what a poor relief!
  For I am ever weeping with my pain,
    And at my weeping laughst thou glad and gay.
      Thus my new tears are fain
      To pay fresh tax of stowre
     When, seen thy laughter, I but weep the more.

## CLVIII.

*Eu me aparto de vós, Ninfas do Tejo,*
(Taking leave of the Lisbon dames. Cf. Sonn. 108).

Nymphs of the Tagus ! I fro' you take flight,
   When least I drad this parting dole to dree ;
   And if in sorrow yede my soul, shall see
Your sight in eyes wherewith I see your sight.
Hopes well-nigh hopeless, plight of utter blight,
   A Love that never sets my Reason free,
   Shall soon bring end to life-long misery,
Save I return to see my dear delight.

But meanwhile never, ne by night ne day,
   Shall thoughts of you be seen depart my heart.
     Love, with me faring, certifies this true.
Whate'er retardance may Return delay,
   One sad companion ne'er fro' me shall part,
     The yearning grief for Weal that bides with you.

## CLIX.

*Vencido esta de Amor*         *Meu pensamento.*
(Acrostic.   " Yours as Captive, highest Senhora !).

| | |
|---|---|
| *Y*ielding to Love I see | *H*igh Thoughts low li'en ; |
| *O*f all Life yielded, all | *I* yielded see, |
| *U*nto you subject, and | *Gi*'en yours to be, |
| *R*endering whate'er I have | *H*ow you design. |
| *S*o well-content I laud | *E*ach moment mine, |
| *A*nd hour when all I saw | *S*urcease to me : |
| *S*ueing a thousand times | *T*he wounds I dree, |

Claiming a thousand more _So_ tristful fine.
_A_ claim so high as this _E_'er shall for-sure
_P_rompt me with Cause to _N_oteworthy prize,
   win
_To_ gain surnatural Height, _H_onour sublime.
_I_ here forswear all _Other_ Aventùre,
_V_owed to a single Love, _R_are sacrifice,
_E_lse by your love to be _A_ttaint of Crime.

## CLX.

_Divina Companhia que nos prados_
(His Exegi Monumentum, &c.).

Ye god-like Bevy who upon the plain
  Of clear Eurotas, or Olympus-Mount,
  Or by the margent of Castalian fount
Holier studies to your heart have tane ;
Sithence the never-movèd Fates ordain
  Me of your number you vouchsafe account,
  In Fame eternal of Bellerophont
To hang these bronze-engravèd verses deign :—

" Soliso (willing future ages note
  How much of Beauty's boon he meriteth
    Who with sage folly doth his soul inflame)
What writ (fro' Fortune now secure) he wrote
  Unto these Altars this hand offereth,
    That hands his Spirit to his beauteous Dame."

## CLXI.

*A la margen del Tajo en claro dia,*
(Spanish : attributed to D. Diogo de Mendoza).

By Tagus' margin on a bloom of day
  With ribbèd ivory combing wavy hair
  Natercia stood, and quencht her eyes the glare
Of nooning Phœbus railing hottest ray.
Soliso, following her in Clytie's way,
  From self far absent while to her full near,
  Sang to his bagpipe praises of his Fere
Who fired his bosom, and thus said his say :—

" If I as many as thy hairs on head
  Had lives to give thee, thou shouldst have the whole,
And pluck them, each and every, thread by thread.
  And for their loss my soul thou wouldst console
If, thousand times as they are numberèd
  In them thou wouldest mesh this life—my sole."

## CLXII.

*Por gloria tuve un tiempo el ser perdido ;*
(Spanish : a Lexapren or repetition Sonnet).

Whilome I gloried to be ruinèd ;
  Ruined me gaining of the purest gain ;
  Gained I when liberty forfared I fain ;
Fain now I find me free but conquerèd.
Conquerèd I to Nisè 'renderèd ;
  'Renderèd lest she leave me lone remain :
  Remain but thoughts of Pleasure turned to Pain ;
Pain gars me now deplore my service sped.

Sped I to serve the Light my love besought ;
  My love besought I hoped to win full sure ;
Full sure my dearest hopes all came to nought.
  Nought of my hope now seems to me secure ;
Security dwelleth but in things ne'er thought ;
  Thought must of dubious end the throes endure.

## CLXIII.

*Rebuelvo en la incessable phantasia,*
(Spanish. Cf. Sonn. No. 77).

I turn and turn in ceaseless Phantasy
  What things I saw when luckiest lot I claimèd,
  Eke when I live (as now) by love inflamèd,
Eke when I livèd from his 'flamings free.
'Twas then mine only thought this fire to flee,
  In life disdaining every shaft he aimèd :
  Now for the Bygones sorrowing and ashamèd
I hold as glory pains I drad to dree.

Right well I recognise 'twas life's delight
  To live a life unrecking doubt and fear,
    When viewed I gust of love as gust of wind.
But now Natercia's spell so charms my sight,
  I find within this jail gloire dearest dear,
    And free to lose it fiercest pain I find.

———

## CLXIV.

*Las peñas retumbavan al gemido*
(Spanish.   Possibly written in Ceuta).

The cliffy mountains echoèd the moan
  Of the sad Shepherd, who vain mourning made
  For griefs that heavy on his spirit weigh'd,
Born of an obstinate Unlove's malison.
The billows ramping on the rocks, each groan
  With hollow tomblings gave rewording aid ;
  'Twas heard confusèd in the winds that stray'd,
'Twas told by dales and vales of caverned stone.

" Respond the hardest Mountains to my grief
Ah me ! (he murmured) rings and roars the Sea,
While woe-full Echoes sympathy confess :
And thou, for whom Death lays his mark on me,
'Sdeignest by hearing grant my pyne relief ;
And when I weep the more I melt thee less.

## CLXV.

*En una selva al dispuntar del dia*
(Spanish.   By Dom Fernando de Acunha ?).

Hid in a forest, at the flush of day,
  Stood sad Endymion wailing for his woes,
  Facing the rays of Sol, who hasty rose
And down a mountain rained his earliest ray.
Fixing the Light that on his joys would prey,
  The Foe who fought to slay his douce repose,
  With sighs and singulfs, these a-following those,
In reasoned sadness thus the swain 'gan say :—

" Clear Light ! obscurest sight I ever view'd,
 Who by thy progress hot and hurrièd
  My Sun obscuredst with thy darkling dyes ;
If aught can move thee in that altitude
 Complaint of Shepherd-youth enamourèd,
  I pray return thee whence thou diddest rise."


## CLXVI.

*Orfeo enamorado que tañia*
(From Monte Mayor's Alcina y Silvano).


The lover Orpheus struck so sweet a quill
 For the lost Ladye he would lief regain,
  Who in implàcable Orcus place had tane,
Thrilled her his harp and voice with tenderest thrill.
Ixion's whirling wheel awhile stood still,
 The tortured Shadows cared not to complain ;
  He gentled every other's harshest pain
And to himself took all of other Ill.

The song prevailèd with so puissant guise,
 That for douce guerdon of his minstrelsy,
  The Kings of Hades (feeling for his woe)
Ordained he fare him with his Fere for prize
 But,—turned that ill-starred wight her sight to see,
  When he and she were lost for evermo'e.

## CLXVII.

*En cantey já, e agora vou chorando*
(The Amores end and begin the Tristia).

I sang in Bygones ; now I weep to see
   The times which heard me sing in faith so fast :
   Meseems when singing in the Days gone past
That tears were gathering in the eyes of me.
I sang ; but an they ask, When mote it be ?
   I n'ote, for even here I was miscast ;
   And now my present state so stands aghast,
Past grief to judgment looks like jubilee.

To sing commanded (traitor Purpose trying)
   Contentment, no ! but Confidence in chance :
     I sang ; yet clank of fetters drowned my song.
Of whom complain when Life is only lying?
   Nay more, why flyte and fleer at Esperance,
     When unjust Fortune more than I did wrong ?

## CLXVIII.

*Ay, Amiga cruel ! que apartamento*
(To the drowned lady. Cf. Sonn. 23, 53, 70, and 99).

Ay, fair and cruel friend ! What sad amiss
   So far from patrial land persuades you stray ?
   Who from the dear nest drives you (well-a-day !)
Glory to eye-glance and to breasts a bliss ?
Fare you a-tempting Fortune's fickleness,
   And of the wilful Winds the fatal fray ?
   Where seas grow coverts ? waves swell hills of spray,
This and that Storm-gust pile upon the abyss ?

But as you leave me thus withouten leaving,
Leave, and may Heaven bestow such aventùre
That all advantage on your hopes attend.
And of this single truth fare right secure,
For this your faring there is more of grieving,
Than wishes wafting you to wisht-for end.

## CLXIX.

*Campo nas Syrtes deste mar da vida,*
(Written at some friend's country house).

Country in shoaling Syrt of Being-sea,
  Safe plank so welcome pluckt from perilous wreck :
  Breaks of calm blue that blackest clouds befleck,
Of Peace the homestead, Love's own sanctuary :
Theeward I fly : but if I win who flee,
  And if a changèd place changed fortunes make,
  Sing me the victor's hymn and in this brake
Honour triumphant o'er all honours be.

When Summer blooms, when Autumn fruitage reaps,
  Here the clear useful waters murmuring flow ;
  Glad finds me here, here gladsome leaves me Day.
Enamoured nightingales here break the sleeps
  Weariness weaveth ; here I 'tomb the Woe
  Whilòm the grave where all my joyaunce lay.

# CLXX.

*Ah, minha Dinamene!   Assi deixaste*
(Ad Dinamenem aquis extinctam.   Cf. Sonn. 168).

Then couldst thou leave, ah Dinamène mine !
   One who could never leave the will to sue thee,
   That now, gent Nymph ! these eyne may ne'er
      review thee ?
Why thus despisèd life so soon resign ?
How couldst abandon for eternal syne
   One who to lose thee did so far pursue thee ?
   And had this Main such might that it withdrew thee
From ever seeing him so doomed to pine ?

Not e'en allowèd me Death dour and dure
   To speak thee, thou thyself the sable veil
      Consentedst o'er thine eyes by Doom be thrown.
O Sea ! O Sky ! O my sad lot obscure !
   What life can lose I that shall much avail,
      If cheap I hold it in such woes to wone !

# CLXXI.

*Guardando em mi a sorte o seu direyto,*
(Same subject.   Garcilasso ; Sonn. 26).

Fortune, preserving rights of sovranty,
   Cut short my gladness when 'twas green and gay.
   Ah me ! how much was ended on that day
Which in my bosom brent such memory !
The more I muse, the more it seemeth me
   That for such welfare Discount one must pay ;
   Unless one deem it meet the World should say
There's perfect goodness in her treacherous gree.

Then if my Fortune for such Discount meant me
.  To dree displeasure, in whose sentiment
Memory can only kill me to content me ;
  What blame shall deal me Thought ? What punish-
    ment ?
If the same cause Thought chooseth to torment me,
  Cause me to suffer ill what Ills torment ?


## CLXXII.

*Cantando estava hum dia bem seguro,*
(Same subject : Lupi Mœrin videre priores).

One day befell me I sang my song secure,
  When Silvio passing this wise said his say :
  (Silvio, that ancient Swain who knew to spae
By song of birds the Future's way full sure.)
" Liso ! whenever willeth Fate obscure,
  Shall come to oppress thee on the self-same day
  Two wolves : at once thy voice and tuneful lay
Shall fly thee, flee thy melody suave and pure ! "

True ! thus it fortunèd ; one tare the throat
Of all I owned, and drove to grass my kine
Whereon I builded hopes of sterling gain.
And for more damage yet, the other smote
My gentle lambkin I did love so fain,
Perpetual yearning of this soul of mine.

## CLXXIII.

*O Ceo, a terra, o vento sossegado;*
(Same subject).

The Heavens and Earth all husht; no gusts to moan;
  The waves dispreading o'er the sandy plain,
  The fishes slumber-reinèd in the Main,
The nightly Silence on her rest-full throne:
The Fisher-youth Aonio, sadly strown
  Where to the wind-breath sways the watery reign,
  Weeps, and the lovèd name bewails in vain,
Which may no longer save by name be known.

"Wavelets! ere Love shall do me dead (he cried)
  To me return my Nymph, whose early Death
    Despite my dolour was by you design'd!"
None answer! Tombleth from afar the tide;
  With gentle movement slow the forest sway'th;
    Winds catch the words and waft them on the
      wind.

## CLXXIV.

*Ah, Fortuna cruel! Ah, duros Fados!*
(Same subject).

Ah cruel Fortune! Ah Fate loath to spare!
  How sudden changed you to the worst my best!
  Your care and cark have robbed me of my rest,
And now ye restfull gloat on cark and care.
Whilere ye made me in fruition fare,
  And your conditions on my gusts would test;
  All, one by one, in single hour to wrest,
Leaving redoublèd bale where blessings were.

How better far had been I never saw
 The doucest boons of Love? Boons (ah!) so suave;
  Why leave me, leaving me of you forlorn?
'Thy voice fro' plaining, peevish Soul! withdraw:
 Soul fallen fro' high estate to pain so grave,
  E'en as thou lovedst in vain 'tis vain to mourn.


## CLXXV.

*Quanto tempo, olhos meus, com tal lamento*
(Probably written in India).

How long, mine Eyes! how long with such lament
 Shall I behold you tristful, aggravated?
  Suffice you not sighs burning, never sated,
Renewing torments aye my soul torment?
Sufficeth not my reveries consent
 In pining, plaining, yearning unabated?
  Still must you fare parforce so ill-entreated
You feed on tear-floods' only nutriment?


I weet not wherefore this Revenge ye take,
 Proving in absence such Repine for pain,
If knew ye all what mote one Esperance make.
 Eyes! other fairest eyes to vex refrain,
'Turning pure love to coy and care-full ache,
 Lest you be chargèd with a coy Disdain.

———

## CLXXVI.

*Lembranças que lembrays o bem passado,*
(Written after Natercia's death?).

Memories remembering Good of by-gone date,
    That present Evil more of ill present,
    Let me, an will ye, live my life content,
Let me not perish in this pitiful state.
If all, withal, be naught but fiat of Fate,
    I die of life in Discontentment spent,
    Come all my blessings by Love's Accident,
And come mine every bane premeditate.

For loss of life to me hath lesser cost,
    As thus 'twould lose sad memories aye memorious,
    Memories whereby such Ills in thought obtain.
For naught he loseth who, in fine, hath lost
    The hopes he cherisht of that good so glorious,
    Which made a pleasure of his very pain.

## CLXXVII.

*Quando os olhos emprégo no passado,*
(Garcilasso, Sonn. I.).

When I employ mine eyes on times gone by,
    Of all my Bygones I parforce repent;
    What went in wanton waste I see misspent;
And all employments misemployed espy.
Aye tied to losing game with tightest tie,
    All I accomplisht 'complisht detriment;
    And recking least what Disillusion meant
When Hope appearèd hopelessest was I.

The many Castles built in dreams of day,
  At point when towering to their tallest pride,
I saw Time sudden on this level lay.
  With what wild Falses wanton Fancy lied !
All stops in Death, the Wind sweeps all away,
  Sad he that hopes ! Sad he that dares confide !


## CLXXVIII.

*Ja cantey, ja chorey a dura guerra*
(A Palinode. Cf. Sonn. 1, 3, 167, 182, and 301).

Erst sang I, erst I wept Love's tyranny,
  And his dure warfare did for years sustain ;
  Forbade he thousand times I tell my bane,
For fear his followers all their error see.
Nymphs ! for whom opes and closes Castaly ;
  Ye who in thousand snares have Death o'ertane,
  Concede me now your energies sovereign,
To tell on Love, what ills encloseth he.

That whoso heed his hest thro' youth's hot tide,
  In my pure verses find a proof full ample
How oft in promised glories hath he lied.
  For while my saddest state I see for sample,
If you inspire my task, full-satisfied
  I'll hang my votive lyre upon your temple.

## CLXXIX.

*Os meus alegres venturosos dias,*
(By Diogo Bernardes?).

My tale of happy, fortune-favoured Days,
  Passed like the leven-ray so speedy spent ;
  Slow-paced fare sluggish stounds of dreariment
Following joyaunce, fugitive estrays.
Ah false pretensions ! Vain phantastick ways !
  What can ye bring me now to breed Content?
  When of my fevered breast the flame that brent
Frore Time to ashes froze that genial blaze.

Past faults in ash-heaps I revolve and trow
Youth left none other fruit for heritage,
Whence shame and Dolour for my soul are meet.
Revolve I more than all my more of age,
Vain longings, vainer weepings, vainest woe,
That fleet-foot Time with all may flit and fleet.

## CLXXX.

*Horas breves de meu contentamento,*
(By Francisco de Sá de Miranda?).

Short Hours ! whose glad Content my fortune gracèd,
  When I enjoyed you, Fancy ne'er had power
  To see you changèd in one easy hour,
And by the tortures of long years effacèd.
What towering castles on the wind I basèd
  O'erturned, in fine, the Wind that bore the tower,
  My fault engendered mine abiding stowre,
For-that on sandy base my house was placèd.

Love with his luring shows at first draws near ;
  All things he maketh possible, all secure ;
But when at bestest then shall disappear.
  Strangest of evils ! strange misaventùre !
For some small good that ne'er can persevere
  One Good to venture that doth aye endure !

## CLXXXI.

*Onde acharey lugar taõ apartado,*
(Written in Africa ?  Cf. Elegy XI.).

Where shall I ever find so far a spot,
  In fullest freedom from all Aventùre,
  I say not only fro' mankind secure,
But e'en where forest-creature entereth not ?
Some dreadful darkling Deene by man forgot,
  Or solitary tangle, sad, obscure,
  Where grow no grasses, flow no fountains pure,
In fine a site so similar to my lot ?

That I, emprisoned in the craggy womb,
May amid Death-in-Life and Life-in-Death,
My fortunes freely and in full lament.
There, as my gauge of grief naught measureth,
No days of joyaunce shall I spend in gloom,
And gloomy days shall find my soul content.

———

## CLXXXII.

*Aqui de longos danos breve historia*
(By Diogo Bernardes ?).

Here of my long-lost Weal short history
　　Who boast them being amourists may read :
　　To them repair of dole it may concede,
Mine it can ne'er fro' memory cause to flee.
I wrote not seeking fame or jactancy
　　My other verses merit for their meed ;
　　But to display her vaunt of cruel deed
Who vaunts so high a victory over me.

Yet grow my sorrows with my growing years,
　　They made my numbers sing, devoid of art,
　　　　The guile of blind-fold Love who robbed my wit.
An voice I gave to song ; I gave to tears
　　My Soul, and tane in hand my pen, this part,
　　　　This little part, of all my pains I writ.

## CLXXXIII.

*Por sua Ninfa Céfalo deixava*
(Of Cephalus the "bucephalous." Ovid., Met. 7).

Cephalus, love-smit by his Nymph withdrew,
　　Leaving Aurora lost in love for aye,
　　Albe the goddess herald lovely Day,
Albe she mirror flowers of rosiest hue.
He who fair Procris loved with love so true,
　　That for her love the world he would bewray,
　　Seeks a temptation that shall try her fay
And tempt the firmness in her Fere she knew.

Doffing his raiment dons he a dire deceit :
   Feigns him another, offers her a price :
      She breaks her fickle faith and gives Consent.
Subtle invention for his own defeat !
   See the blind lover find so strange device
      That live he ever life of Discontent !


## CLXXXIV.

*Sentindose alcançada a bella Esposa*
(Continues Sonn. 183.   Where is the third ?).


Feeling herself entrapt the lovely Spouse
   Of Cephalus to sin so readily led,
      Far from her husband o'er the mountains fled,
By snare compelled or by shame none trows.
For he, in fine, whom jealous pangs arouse
   And on blind errand by Cupido sped,
      Like a lost traveller toileth on her tread
And pardoneth all her crimes of violate vows.

Before the hard Nymph's feet he prostrate lay,
   Who for his jealous trick enstoned her heart,
To pray her pardon, e'en for life to pray.
   Oh strong Affection with thy madding art !
When for the sin that would himself betray
   He must pray pardon from the peccant part !

———

## CLXXXV.

*Seguia aquelle fogo que o guiava,*
(After Musæus).

Followed the beckoning of the beacon-fire
  Leander, battling wind and battling wave ;
  Yet brast the billows on the breast so brave
The more, as Love would more of strength inspire.
Whenas his forces felt he faint and tire,
  Without one craven thought his will to enslave,
  Tho' reft of words, the intent for which he strave
Thus he commended to the sea's deaf ire :—

" Thou Sea !" (the youngling cried in lone distress)
My life I pray not ; now my only prayer
Save me my Hero, nill this sight she see.
Bear thou my lifeless body, let it fare
Far from her tower ; be my friend in this
Sith my best joyaunce moved thy jealousy.

## CLXXXVI.

*Os olhos onde o casto Amor ardia,*
(Epitaph-sonnet, by Diogo Bernardes ?).

Those eyne where showed chaste Love his ardent glow,
  Joying his fiery form in them to sight ;
  That face where blusht with lustre marvel-bright
The Rose-bud purpling on her bed of snow :
The locks that fired Sol with envious lowe
  Because they 'minishèd his golden light ;
  That hand's pure whiteness and that form so dight
In clay Death-chillèd all lie here below.

Perfectest loveliness in youngest years,
  Blossom in time untimely torn from Earth,
That fades and withers gript by Death's hand dure :
  How melts not Love and drowns in piteous tears?
Not shed for Her who fared to heavenly birth ;
  But for himself left here in night obscure.


## CLXXXVII.

*Ditosa pena, como a maõ que a guia,*
(To Manvel Barata the Caligrapher : after A.D. 1572).


Pen ! ever happy as its guiding hand,
  With such perfected art in subtlest ways,
  Whenas with Reason I would 'tempt thy praise,
I lose the praises which my Fancy fand :
But Love, who shifteth efforts at command,
  Command to sing thee all-wise on me lays,
  Not with the warrior-plectrum Mart essays,
But in suave melodies and musick bland.

Thy name, Emmanuel hight, from Pole to Pole
  Sublimely towereth spreading thy renown,
    When erst none raisèd thee above thy peers :
But that thy name be writ on deathless roll ;
  Behold Apollo brings the bloomy crown,
    Kept as thy guerdon for such growth of years.

## CLXXXVIII.

*Espanta crecer tanto o Crocodilo,*
(To a new bishop, Pinheiro, the Pine.  Cf. Sonn. 190).

We note with marvel growth of Crocodile
  Only for born so puny-impotent ;
  Who, born a grosser birth, would represent
A lesser marvel to his patrial Nyle.
Vainly shall heavenward raise my earthly style
  Your new and now Pontifical ornament ;
  For deathless Merits, while a-womb still pent
Shaped robes to enrobe you in the welcome while.

Foreslow'd yet slow it came : our due of meed
Oft cometh slowest ; this is sure and clear,
Tho' guerdon some time cometh not remiss.
The spheres, that nearest neighbour Primal Sphere,
Have tardier movements.  Who hath power to rede
Upon that riddle, riddle such as this !

## CLXXXIX.

*Ornou sublime esforço a o grande Atlante,*
(To the Viceroy D. Joam de Castro).

Bedeckt great Atlas meed of Might sublime,
  Wherewith the sky-machine he mote sustent ;
  Genius enhonoured Homer to invent
'Yond the fourth sky a path for Greece to climb.
Crownèd clear constant Love who spurneth Time :
  Orpheus, ne peace could tempt ne storm torment ;
  Inspirèd Fortune free and confident
Cæsar, her fondling in his youthful prime.

Thou, Fame ! upraisedst to the hill of Gloire
   Alcide in ranges where thou lovst to bide :
      But Castro, Heaven-endowed with highest claim,
Decks, honours, crowns, inspires, upraises more
   Than Atlas, Homer, Orpheus, Cæsar, Alcide,
      The meed of Might, Genius, Love, Fortune,
      Fame.

## CXC.

*Despoys que vio Cibele o corpo humano*
(Cf. Sonn. 188).

When viewèd Cybelè what erst had been
   Fair Atys' human form grown verdant Pine,
   Her first vain anger gan to ruth incline,
And hopeless wailèd she her new-born teen.
Devising noble snare her woe to wean,
   She prayèd Jupiter, of love divine,
   The worth of noble Palm and Bay to assign
Unto her Pine-tree, Sovran of the Green.

Vouchsafes a better boon her puissant Son,
   Its growth should touch the stars with towering
      brow,
   And there see mysteries of the sky supernal.
O happy Pine-tree ! O thou happier one
   Who sees his brows becrownèd with your bough
      And in your shadow sings his songs eternal !

## CXCI.

*Poys torna por seu Rey, e juntamente*
(To Viceroy D. Luis de Athaide in 1577).

Then for his Roy to rule, and service do
    For Christ conjointly, 'turneth to the part
    Where self he showed a Numa and a Mart,
Enfamèd Lewis just and valiant-true :
Let Tagus hope all Orient-land to view
    (Where rarely gifts so rare the Heavens impart)
    Yielding to such high force, such prudent art,
Of Palms a thousand, thousand tributes new.

Whoso of Ganges or of Indus drink,
    Whom scant availèd strength of spear or shield,
        Shall bow and bowing have the lesser harm.
Hearing his coming name shall Eùphrate shrink ;
    Foreseeing all things to his terror yield,
        As erst seen conquered by his forceful arm.

## CXCII.

*Agora toma a espada, agora a pena,*
(To Estacio de *Faria ;* Soldier and Poet).

Now hends in hand the Brand, now hends the Pen
    Our Eustace either gift hath glorified,
    Being or Mars-beloved on briny tide
Or Muse's lover in sweet-founted glen.
Sonorous Swan, fair Riverside's denizen !
    To sing thine exploits were my joy and pride ;
    For song deserving thee was aye denied
To rustick pipe or reed of rural men.

If I who hent the Pen and hent the Brand,
  To play with either mote permission claim,
    By the high influence Planets twain award;
With this and other light by their command,
  Thou, man of pushing arm and soul of flame!
    Shalt fare a Pharos-lamp to Brave and Bard.


## CXCIII.

*Erros meus, má Fortuna, Amor ardente*
(The Penitent poems begin).


Mine Errors, evil Fortune, Amor's lowe
  Did for the spilling of my life conspire:
    O'ermuch was error, vain was Fortune's ire,
Sufficed me only Love and nothing mo'e.
I passed them all, but now so present show
  Of Things that passèd Dolours dure and dire,
    Their long persistence taught me all Desire
To lose, for longing no Content can know.

I erred through all the courses of my years;
  I lent to Fortune prètext to chastise
    My hopes ill-founded on a foot so frail.
Little I saw of Love save passing snares.
  Ah had I power to glut in fellest guise
    With its revenge this Spirit hard to quail!

## CXCIV.

*Cá nesta Babilonia a donde mana*
(First Zion-Babylon-Goa Sonnet.  Cf. Psalm 136).

Here in this Babylon-realm, where rails amain
  Matter which breeds a World's iniquity :
Here, where the purest Love hath low degree,
Whose Mother's more of might makes all prophane :
Here where Bad grows a blessing, Good a bane ;
  Where Might is Right and Right is Tyranny :
Here where a blind and blundering Monarchy
Holds God deceived by verbiage empty-vain :

Here in this Labyrinth where the Good, the Wise,
  The noblest bred to beg their bread are met
Before the gates of villein covetize :
  Here in this Chaos black with fume and fret,
I wend the natural way before me lies.
  See then if thee, my Zion ! I can forget !

## CXCV.

*Correm turbas as agoas deste rio,*
(His Country's disorder : an allegory).

Turbid the waters of our River glide,
  Befouled by freshets and bestained by rain :
  Drowth wilts the flowerage of the riant plain
And wuthering winds thro' withering Valleys gride
Passèd (like Winter) ardent Summer-tide ;
  These things for others in exchange were tane :
  The faithless Fates retirèd from the Reign
Of worldly matters to misrule affied.

Now Time his order to ordain hath known ;
Not so the World : It courseth so askance
That all its semblance showeth God-forgot.
Nature, opinions, habit, various chance
So work that seemeth all the life we own
Is but a semblance, what seems not *is* not.

## CXCVI.

*Vósoutros que buscays repouso certo*
(Same theme as Sonn. 350).

Ye other Wanderers seeking certain rest
  In life, by divers deeds of enterprise ;
  To whom, on worldly gear enfixing eyes,
A veil would seem its governance to invest ;
Offer to Disconcèrt (an deem ye best)
  Your new-born honours, blinded sacrifice ;
  For àntique vices fitly to chastise
God wills the course of things His rule attest.

Ne'er in such form of chastisement he fell
  Who blameth Fortune, to believe content
    That Sort and Chances form Creation's plan.
In great experience greater dangers dwell :
  But what God seeth just and evident,
    Seemeth unjust and over-deep for man.

## CXCVII.

*Para se namorar do que criou,*
(Conception Sonnet : Petrarch II. Canz. 8).

To love the Made, with loving infinite
    God made Thee, holy Phœnix, purest Maid !
    Behold how great must be the Creature's grade
Whom the Creator hath for self bedight !
He framed thy substance in ideal height
    Prime, ere Creation's primal base was laid ;
    That be unique in own array array'd
The Made, long studied by the Maker's might.

I n'ote that any words of mine can own
    Power to express those rarest qualities
In thee He made whom madest thou thy Son.
Daughter, Wife, Mother, Thou ! and if hast won
    Thou singly three such lofty dignities,
'Twas Thou, sole Thou, so pleasedst the Three-in-
    One.

## CXCVIII.

*Dece do Ceo immenso Deos benino,*
(Incarnation Sonnet : Amœbæan).

Descends from Heaven's immense the God benign,
    Made flesh in Maiden-mother sovereign.
    Why downs the power Divine to dwell with men ?
"'Tis that Mankind uprise to the Divine."
Why comes he then so poor and infantine
    Bearing the baleful power of tyrant-bane ?
    "'Tis that He comes Death's bitter cup to drain
And pay of senseless Adam's sin the fine."

Then could the Twain dare eat that fruit of tree,
The food their Maker so to them forbade?
" Yes ; for they sought assume Divinity."
And for this reason was He human made?
" Yes ; for 'twas ordered, and with cause obey'd,
If man would be a god, God man should be."


## CXCIX.

*Dos Ceos à terra dece a mór Belleza ;*
(Nativity Sonnet : quasi-Amœbæan).

Fro' Heaven the highest Beauty earthward flies,
    And with our flesh ennobled deigneth wone ;
    That Man by Povert erst so woe-begone
This day to richest riches mote arise.
The wealthiest Lord doth poorest penury prize ;
    For when to mortal world His love was shown,
    That tender body on vile straw was strown,
And for this straw Heaven's self He doth despise.

" How? God descend on Earth in Poverty?"
    That which is poorest gars Him so content,
Seems such Contentment Earth's sole treasury.
    This manger Poverty doth represent ;
But so great merit Povert rose to be,
    Content him most the pauperest indigent.

——— ,

## CC.

*Porque a tamanhas penas se offerece.*
(Passion Sonnet: quasi-Amœbæan).

Why Self thus offereth to such penalty
    For sin of alien, error so insane,
    The trinal Godhead? " 'Tis because the pain
Due to his punishment no man can dree."
Say, who shall suffer all that suffereth He?
    Who shall endure dishonour death and bane?
    "Who be so potent, save the Sovereign
Which reigns and rules His slaves obediently?

Man's highest power had so puny might,
It lackt the puissance with such stowre to fence,
Nor kept the laws ordainèd by the Lord.
Yet all He suffered by that Strength immense
In cause of purest love; for aye propense
Sin-ward our weakness was, not sin's award.

## CCI.

*Depoys de aver chorado os meus tormentos,*
(A Proëmium to the Tristia).

When I had wept, bewailing my despair,
    Love wills me sing the glories of his prize.
I sing the victories of a fairest Faire,
    And of long-suffering weep the Memories.
But an those pains of mine be victories
    In such a cause when Thought so high shall fare;
Dispread themselves in large large histories
    These my surrenders that such boast can bear.

Let one sole marvel make the Universe ring,
   What be her beauties at whose shrine I bow,
Who pays with fee of tears the songs I bring.
   Content I offer Love this tax of woe :
For an no sobs can match the song I sing,
   No singing sweeter than these sobs I know.


## CCII.

*Onde merecí eu tal pensamento,*
(The same theme).

Whence did I merit by such Thought be shent,
   Never by human being merited?
   Whence did I merit to be conquerèd
Of one whose conquest so high honour lent?
Grows to a glory what did most torment,
   When seeing showeth me to loss misled;
   For no such evil was in hardihead
As there was glory in that hardiment.

I live, my Ladye, only while I view you ;
   And so this soul surrenders to the strife
     That, drowned in tears, I take of life my leave.
But ne'er shall make my spirit cease to lo'e you
   Fears of my losing in your cause my life,
     For you a thousand-fold of lives I'd give.

## CCIII.

*De frescas belvederes rodeadas*
(To certain Maids of Honour at Cintra).

By bents encircled, blooming green and gay,
    Pour the pure waters flowing fro' this fount ;
    And throngs of beauteous Nymphs take stand afront
Aye wont to conquer and the foe to slay.
They raise, these Rebels spurning Cupid-sway,
    Their grace and graces lacking tale and count :
    Forgetting other valley, other mount,
And here in quiet while their lives away.

Summoned his powers and donned his bravest mood
    Love, who no longer mote endure the slight,
        Only to make the Mays his vengeance know.
But when he saw them, straight he understood
    From death or prison lacked he power of flight,
        And there with them he 'bode without his bòw.

## CCIV.

*Nos braços de hum Silvano adormecendo*
(To Belisa, who married a Bestial for his wealth).

Bound to a Sylvan's breast a-slumbering lay,
    And there remained, the Nymph I do adore.
        Paying lip-tribute in so sugrèd store,
Whereby a darkness robbed my eyes of day.
O lovely Venus ! Why this patience, pray,
    Suffering thy beauteous Choir's most beauteous
        flower,
    So lose her honour in so vile a power,
When highest merit fails her fee to pay ?

As predetermined I henceforth will trow,
  Seeing what novel strangest freak thou bravest,
    In thee can nothing sure or true endure.
Since the clear luminous cheek, the lovely brow
  To that misformèd monstrous Thing thou gavest,
    I'll hold Love nothing—only Aventùre.


## CCV.

*Quem diz que Amor he falso, ou enganoso,*
(A defence of pure Love).


Who calls Love felon, lief of tricks and lies;
  Of legier mind, forgetful, vain, ingrate,
    Shall find withouten fail his merited Fate
A rule of rigour, rife of cruelties.
Love be douce-minded, charged with charities;
  Who saith contrayr allow his words no weight;
    Let him be judgèd blind and passionate,
Let men detest him and the gods despise.

That Love works Evil well in me is seen;
In me his rigour shows right rigorous showing,
To show the World how long his reach and range:
But all Love's angers still with love are glowing:
And all his evils I for welfare ween
Nor would for other weal such teen exchange.

———

## CCVI.

*Fermosa Beatriz, tendes taes geitos*
(To a Dame of low degree? Cf. Sonn. 69).

Beautiful Beatrice ! such 'luring geste
　　In the soft roving of those orbs you show,
　　That not to linger, but one look to throw
Inflames the heart and burns the human breast.
All your perfections be so perfectest,
　　Such bliss to merit Hope we must forego,
　　Nor can their knowledge come for man to know
Without enduring Cupid's dure behest.

Felt, to my sorrow, so grave blight and bane
These eyes, that seeing those with sadness blind,
Lost all their pleasure wi' the light forlore.
But now you've dealt with them hurt so unkind,
Look with humaner eyes on me again
And to my hurt you shall full health restore.

## CCVII.

*Alegres campos, verdes, deleitosos,*
(To Ignez in the Coimbra country?).

Glad meadows ! gaily deckt with greeny dyes,
　　Your pretty Days-eyes aye these eyne shall woo,
　　For-that their beauties did themselves enmew
In babes of fair Ignèz' all-beauteous eyes.
Fro' mine, that ever gaze in envious guise,
　　When stars so godlike I no more may view,
　　Ye shall be watered with another dew,
Ye shall be airèd by a lover's sighs.

And ye, gold-petaled flowers ! peraventure
If wish and will Ignèz my love to essay
With trial tested to the latest leaf :
Show her, that she approve a faith so pure,
Fair flowers ! *He-loves-me* (and shall love for aye)
That of the *Loves-me-not* I 'scape the grief.

## CCVIII.

*Ondados fios de ouro, onde enlazado*
(To a dame named Paz, *i.e.* Peace ?).

Ye rippling golden Threads ! whose tangled skein
  My thoughts for ever in your meshes hold,
  The more fresh breezes loose you fold by fold,
More am I prisoner of my present pain.
Love, always armèd with some beauteous eyne,
  Fights me by force of tormentise untold,
  Proving the sufferings in my soul ensoul'd,
When I to justest laws of Peace incline.

Thus in your lovely, more than mortal geste
  I love conjoinèd Peace and parlous fray ;
And loving this and that unsnared I rest :
  With self I còmmune, and full oft I say
When such the cause is of my care and quest,
  Just is the warfare, just the Peace I pray.

## CCIX.

*Amor, que em sonhos vãos do pensamento*
(Attributed to F. R. I. Surrupita).

Love who in vainest dreams of phantasy
  Pays greater jealousy he would abate,
  Made me in all conditions, every state,
The tributary of his tormentry.
I slave, I weary ; yet my due degree
  For sacrifice to Love-shrine consecrate,
  Scattered in atomies by hands ingrate,
Eterne Oblivion robbed eternally.

But when o'er much, in fine, the perils grow
  Whereto condemneth me without surceàse
Love, not my lover, rather Love my foe ;
  Fro' pain I ever find one grand release,
For gloire of loving, which I ne'er forego,
  No force of evils ever can decrease.

## CCX.

*Nem o tremendo estrepito da guerra,*
(Written at Ceuta after losing an eye ?  Cf. Canz. IX. 3).

Not the tremendous clash and clang of fight
  With fire and fatal arms the world affray,
  And drive the deadly bullets in such way
They threaten overthrow to serrièd height,
Have power the fearless lover to affright,
  Sin' flashed thy fairest eyne their fitful ray,
  Whereby such horrors wi' their dire dismay,
Fade from my senses and are fain of flight.

Life I can lavish, or by burn or brand,
  In any dreadful danger bid it go,
And (Phœnix-like) fro' death fresh life command.
  For me no mister evil fate I know,
Wherefrom I may not free me out of hand,
  Save from what orders Love, Love aye my foe.


## CCXI.

*Fiouse o coraçao, de muyto isento,*
(Addressed to some kinswoman ; loved not honestly ?).


The heart entrusted self erst Fancy-free
  To self; ill recking that a heart could hold
  Love so illicit, love so daring-bold,
.Such mode of torment man may never see.
Yet did these eyne so limn in Phantasy
  Others beheld in fancies manifold,
  That Reason, dreading all she did behold,
Leaving the field to Thought was fain to flee.

O chaste Hippolytus ! in similar plight
  Thy stepdame Phædra sought thy love to gain,
Rejecting all respect for wrong and right ;
Love thy chaste bosom 'vengèd on my sprite :
  But Love such vengeance by this brunt hath tane
He now repents him of the deed he dight.

———

## CCXII.

*Quem quiser ver de Amor huma excellencia,*
(Written before a parting?   Petrarch, I. 210).

Whoso would see of Love an excellence,
　Where delicacy doth all love depure,
　Mark he where placèd me mine Aventure,
That of my faith he find experience.
Where long-drawn Absence slayeth Sovenance,
　On the dread ocean-wave, in warfare dure,
　Growth of love-yearnings groweth more secure
Where Patience runneth risk of more mischance.

But place me Fortune mine or hard-heart Fate
　In Death, perdition, sorest bane and scathe,
　　Or raise to prosperous post, to highmost height.
Place me, for short, in lowest, loftiest state,
　They still shall find I hold till bitter death
　　One name a-lip, and one pure face a-sprite.

## CCXIII.

*Los ojos que con blando movimiento*
(Spanish : written *a voluntad ajena ?*).

Those eyne whose gentle glances sweetly bent
　My spirit soften as they stray and play,
　　Vouchsafed they dwell with me one single day
Well mote their magick make my Woes relent.
By power of fondest-loving sentiment
　Mine importuning Ills would end for aye ;
　　Or would their Accident such growth display
That Life had ended in a twinkling spent.

Ah ! did thy coyness not to me deny
  Thy visioned charms, O Nymph thou loveliest,
The hand-work of thine eyes had done me die !
  Oh, would they linger at thy will ! How blest
Would be the moment when I mote espy
  My life in them restored, restored my rest !


## CCXIV.

*No bastava que Amor puro, y ardiente,*
(Spanish : two deaths to his life, his love and her hate).


Was't not enough that Love, who purely brent,
  With these conditions hath my life efface'd ;
  But e'en must Death and Doom in hottest haste
Deal me such unhumànest accident ?
My Soul ne'er claimed, though much she may resent,
  To cut the rigorous course that Love has trace'd,
  That mote She never die nor ever taste
Unlove of what she loved with sweet intent.

But your strong Will, that can all Wills defeat
  With these your graces, deigned for me ordain
    Harshness impossible, unheard, unknown :
That scornful ague and Love's fever-heat
  Of ire, with single blow fro' me have tane
    One life by two-fold different Deaths o'erthrown.

———

## CCXV.

*Ayudame, Senora, a ser venganҫa*
(Spanish : by D. Manoel de Portugal ?).

Aid me, my Ladye! some revenge to wreak
  On Sprite so savage, mind so rude, so base,
  Sithence my scanty worth, my lowly case
To thee dared soar, and hope of thee bespeak :
To this Perfection thine we vainly seek,
  To these thy heights sublime of charms and grace,
  Where Nature raised her once to pride of place,
But where to rise once more her trust is weak.

Whatso in thee I contemplate so lieve,
With contemplation lacking thy consent,
More contemplating less of hope I 'joy.
If thou to revel in my pains be bent
Rain on me wrath, deign Love with Unlove grieve
I lo'e thee more the more thou workest annoy.

## CCXVI.

*O claras aguas deste blando rio,*
(Spanish : by Diogo Ramires Pagan ?).

Clear-welling waters of this stilly rill,
  Whose mirror painteth in their natural dyes
  Frondiferous graces spireing to the skies
From blurred forest based on swelling hill.
So ne'er cold Rain-storm, never South-wind chill
  Perturb the picture in their turbid guise,
  For to preserve them e'en through summer dries
I will their wastage with these tears refill.

And when Marfisa views my form in you,
　　Then may my figure, lorn of life and light,
　　　　To her clear eyesight framed and formèd be ;
And if she would for me your view unview,
　　(Showing my sight offends her) may her sight
　　　　On pain of seeing me not, herself not see.


## CCXVII.

*Mil vezes entre sueños tu figura,*
(Spanish : by Francisco de Sá de Miranda ?).


Amid a thousand dreams thy portraiture
　　(O lovely Nymph !) I viewed with clearest eye ;
　　　　And, more desiring as I more espy,
Fro' dreams I'd wake to 'joy its formosure :
While this my Dreamery's sweetness shall endure,
　　In vain possession's barren boast live I :
　　　　But when my bold Desire would soar so high,
It wakes, falls plat and cowers in shade obscure.

I grieve at waking for the sight o' thee ;
　　And, tho' my sight to unsee may please thee most,
I'd lief go blind to see the light o' thee ;
　　But if by sleight I must maintain my post,
And Love would lose me by despight o' thee,
　　Sans gain the greatest I may not be lost.

## CCXVIII.

*Mi Gusto y tu Beldad se desposaron,*
(Spanish : this by Camoens, or by Dr. Ayres Pinel ?).

My Gust thy Beauty made a covert-feme,
  Mine Eyes, for greater ill, being Go-between :
  And such the joyaunce of the twain hath been,
They bore a lovely bairn and Love his name.
Both spoilèd him in mode so misbecame
  That, when their happiness seemèd most serene,
  Scant understanding what the loss could mean,
Lost by their love they found them, Sire and Dame.

But Beauty marrièd in such fallacy,
  Brought forth a two-winged monster of appal ;
And Pride, his father, 'gat Childe Jealousy.
  O Father equal to thy Son in all !
Who gars the immortal Grandsire mortal be
  And gives the mortal Sire immortal Hall ?

## CCXIX.

*Si el fuego que me inciende, consumido*
(Spanish.  Cf. Eclogue V. 36–7).

An the fierce flames that fire me could be laid
  By some Aquarius of a sprite more spry ;
  An I were changèd by the sighs I sigh
To air dispersèd through the airy stead ;
If hearing horrible sounds of dread, my dread
  Could 'fright my spirit from my flesh to fly ;
  Or sea receive from ever-weeping eye
A body molten by the tears it shed ;

Never could irous Fortune so illude
  (With every terror horrible and fere)
    My sprite, and all her glory from her rive.
For in your Beauty she is merged, transmew'd,
  Nor all the tears that trill to Stygian mere
    Could fro' my memory either boast outdrive.

## CCXX.

*Que me quereys, perpétuas saudades ?*
(Portuguese : the Tristia again.  Cf. Sonn. 93).

Of me what seek you, Thoughts that alway yearn ?
  What are the snaring Hopes you hold in store ?
    Time who once fleeth shall return no more
And if return he, Youth may not return.
Years ! a good reason for your flight we learn
  For-that so lightsome, lightly pass ye o'er ;
    Nor all are equal in one flavour, nor
Shall Will for ever things conform discern.

The friend I lovèd erst is now so changèd
  Well nigh to other ; for the Days this wise
The gusts of youthtide damaged and derangèd.
  Hopes of new pleasures, joys of novel guise,
Nor Fortune granteth, nor doth Time estrangèd,
  Who of Content and Happiness are the spies.

## CCXXI.

*Oh rigurosa ausencia desejada*
(Spiritus promptus est, &c.   Petrarch, I. 174).

O rigorous Absence I so longed to see
  And ever longed for while 'twas all unknown !
  Longings so fearèd in the days long flown,
As now experienced to my misery !
Already you 've begun right rigorously
  To press your hopes of doing my life undone ;
  You do so much, I fear that woe-begone
Hope, with my Life opprest, shall cease to be.

The Days most gladsome bring me saddest wail ;
  The Nights in sorrow watch I and discompt ;
Sans you appear they sans accompt or tale.
  I wait a-famished, and the years accompt ;
Natheless with life of me, in fine, they fail ;
  Nor for my flesh infirm my Soul is prompt.


## CCXXII.

*Ay ! quien dará a mis ojos una fuente*
(Spanish : Jeremiah's Quis dabit, &c.   Ch. 9).

Ah ! Who shall give a fountain to these eyne,
  A fount of tear-flood flowing night and day ?
  Perchance my Soul had found some rest and stay
In weeping passèd time and present syne.
Ah ! Who shall lend me place apart to pine,
  Tracking my Dolour's trail in obstinate way,
  With tristful Memories and the Phantasy
O' Weal that fathered such an Ill as mine !

Ah ! Who shall give me words to express the spight,
  The hard Unlove which Love for me hath wrought,
Where Patience scantly can avail my plight ?
  Ah ! Who shall bare my bosom's veilèd thought ?
Where is the Secret writ that shuns the light,
  The hidden sorrows all my life have fraught ?


## CCXXIII.

*Con razon os vays, aguas, fatigando*
(Spanish : by the Marquess of Astorga ?).

With reason, Waters ! do ye toil and tire
  A glad reception's boon and bourne to gain
  And reach the bosom of that boundless Main
Whereto so many days your hopes aspire.
Harrow ! Whose sorrows aye weep Fortune's ire,
  Lost hopes of vanities the vainest vain ;
  And with the dolours of that tearful rain
Ne'er find, in fine, the goal of fond Desire.

Ye the directest way-line ever spurning,
  Fail not the wisht-for scope and end to make,
  Howe'er embarrasst by the random round.
But I, through night and day with grief aye yearning !
  Albe one pathway I may ne'er forsake,
  The wisht-for Haven never never found.

## CCXXIV.

*O cesse ya, Señor, tu dura mano !*
(Spanish : Cf. Canzon IV. 4).

Lighten at length, Lord Love, that heavy hand !
Nor drive my life to Life's extreme despight.
Suffice so wasted bides it by thy might
Not one sound passage may in it be scann'd.
Ah, strangest Formosure ! Ah, fere command
Of Fate inhuman aye forbidding flight !
An of compassion be deprived thy sprite
Snapt thou shall see, soon see, my vital strand.

A bland Unlove, a Love as blandly fair,
For one so utter lost were fit, were meet
For one who ne'er may hope his Ill to guarish.
And if to see how fare I scant thou care,
Behold me here surrenderèd at thy feet.
Flourish thy Fancy ; Go, my Hope ! go perish.

## CCXXV.

*Dulces engaños de mis ojos tristes ;*
(Spanish : to a likeness of his lover ?).

Ye douce Delusions of my doleful eyes,
What lively sense of Thought in me ye awake !
That only presence my Content could make
You turn to shadowy Painture's shadowy dyes.
You have entender'd with a soft surprise
My feelings mastered by a sudden quake ;
Yet not one moment for your promise sake
Those vainly profferèd boons you made my prize.

I saw the figure was a counterfeit,
　　Not hers who hideth in herself my Soul,
　　Tho' here it rival with the natural :
This wise it hears my sighs, thus answers it ;
　　Thus with my wasted life it doth condole,
　　As though the copy were the original.


## CCXXVI.

*Quanto tiempo ha que lloro un dia triste,*
(Spanish : written during the first exile ?).


How long one tristful day shall I bewail
　　As though I hopèd joy my life to cheer ?
　　How is it, Tagus ! whenas course thy clear
Waters, thou dyedst them not my life to swale ?
Veiling my path thou dost my breast unveil,
　　O my sad Fortune of my weal so near !
　　Adieu ye Mounts of rarest beauty sheer ;
Adieu my heart that may not burst for bale.

If, where thou dwellest lief and lot-content,
　　Thou hadst not drunk a draught of Lethe-drain,
　　In so much Weal such Woes were not forgot.
Singing my Dolours shall my death lament ;
　　For e'en the senseless Hill with hollow strain
　　Soundeth hoarse accents to console my lot.

## CCXXVII.

*Levantay, minhas Tagides, a frente,*
(To Dom Theodosio. Cf. Sonn. 20).

High raise your glorious brows, my Tagidès!
  Leaving where Tagus forest-shaded flows:
  Gild ye the rory vale, the dewy rose
And hill-side hairy with the hanging trees.
Awhile in absence leave your river-leas;
  Cease with the numbered verse the lyre to arouse:
  Cease all your labours, Nymphs of formous brows!
Cease the full current from your fountain flees.

Speed ye to greet Theodosio great and clear,
  To whom in offering of sublimer song
    On golden harp fair-faxt Apollo sings.
Minerva lends him (rarest meed) her lere;
  Pallas lends Valour which adaws the throng;
    And Fame fro' Pole to Pole his rumour wings.


## CCXXVIII.

*Vôs Ninfas da Gangetica espessura*
(To the Captain D. Leoniz Pereira, in 1568).

You Nymphs who grace Gangetick coverture!
  In voice sonorous deign sweet praise to outpour
  For the high captain, whom the rosy Aurore
Saved from the tarnisht sons of Night obscure.
Mustered the Negro-hordes who, dour and dure,
  Lord it on Aurea-Chersonesian shore,
  From dearest nide to outdrive for evermore
Men who in might excel Misaventure.

But a strong Lyon, with small company,
 The mighty Manye, fon as fere in fight,
  Defeated, 'feebled, punisht and unmann'd.
Nymphs ! sing ye joyous songs, for clear you see
 More than Leonidas for Græcia dight
  Did noble Leoniz in Malàca-land.


## CCXXIX.

*Alma gentil, que á firme Eternidade*
(On Dom A. de Noronha. Cf. Sonn. 12).


Gent Soul ! that unto firm Eternity
 By valour rising, home for aye didst make,
  Here shall endure, and Memory ne'er forsake,
Our pain and pine with name and fame of thee.
I n'ote if in such Youth more wonderous be
 To leave man jealous for thy valour's sake ;
  Or if an Adamant-breast, or tooth of Drake,
Thou hadst compelled to pay Compassion's fee.

Jealous of thine a thousand lots I view,
While mine is jealouser than all the rest,
For-that my loss thy loss thus equalleth.
Oh happy dying ! Sort so sadly blest !
What thousand ordinary deaths ne'er do
Thou didst with derring-do of one fair Death.

———

## CCXXX.

*Debaxo desta pedra, sepultada*
(Epitaph on Dona Caterina?).

She lies ensepulchred below this stone
  Whose noblest beauty was a World-delight ;
  Whom Death of merest envy and despight,
From Life-tide robbèd ere her day was done ;
Nowise respecting her, that paragon
  Of gentlest radiance, who the gloomiest night
  Turned into clearest noon ; whose whitest light
Eclipst the clearest splendours of the Sun.

Truly Sol bribèd thee, thou cruel Death !
  To set him free fro' radiance gart him gloom ;
    Bribed thee the Moon who paled before her ray.
How haddest thou such power to rob her breath ?
  And, if thou haddest, how so soon couldst doom
    A World-light fade and vade to death-cold clay ?

## CCXXXI.

*Imagens vãas me imprime a Fantasia ;*
(By the Infant Dom Luiz ?).

In me vain fancies Fancy would inlay ;
  Novel discourses all my Thoughts invent ;
  And more my woe-wrung Spirit to torment
Cares of a century pack in single day.
Had Thought high object, sooth it were to say
  Hope might discover on what base she lent :
  But Fate ne'er courses with so true intent
The rights of Reason she will deign to weigh.

Chance led by Fortune oftentimes succeedeth ;
But an, peraunter, deal they boons victorious
Favour of Fame for falsehood is notorious.
Determination Wisdom's worth exceedeth :
Only by constancy man groweth glorious :
Only free Souls are digne to be memorious.


## CCXXXII.

*Quanta incerta esperança, quanto engano !*
("Catholic verities").

How much of doubtful Hope, how sly a snare !
  How much of Life in lying reverie spent !
  For all fare building with the same intent
Only on bases where to loss they fare :
They strive thro' doubtful human life to steer ;
  They trust in words that be mere windy vent ;
  Then through long hours and moments they lament
The gladdest laughter of a live-long year.

Ne'er let Appearance worth of aught enhance ;
  Intend that Life is but a borrowed store ;
For the world liveth in a change of chance.
  Then change thy sentiments, be thy care forlore,
And aye love only that one Esperance
  Which with the Lovèd One lasts evermore.

———

## CCXXXIII.

*Mal, que de tempo em tempo vas crecendo ;*
(By the Infante Dom Luis ?).

Ills ! that fro' time to time so crescive grow ;
   Would by one Good I saw you 'companied !
Then should my life-term in repose abide,
Nor feel one fear to sight Death's horrid show.
If man his petty cares to sighs of woe
   Convert, and if the sighs new cares provide,
   Ah me how prudent ! O how fortified
Weaving his bay-wreath he thro' life shall go !

'Tis time we unremember past Content,
   Past with the hopes of joyaunce ever past,
And overtriumph'd by a new Intent :
   May living Faith, that holds my Spirit fast,
To caduque derring-do a term present
   Whereto past Welfare doomed itself at last.

## CCXXXIV.

*O quanto melhor he o supremo dia,*
(Cupio dissolvi, &c.).

O how far better man's supremest Day,
   Douce day of death, than birth-tide's bitter boon !
   O how far better is the moment's swoon
That ends so many a year of agony !
Cease to seek other Weals in stubborn way :
   Cease all applièd end of Thoughts high-flown,
   Of all that gives contentment one alone
Man's flesh contents, his couch of death-cold clay.

Who doth the Godhead as his steward hold,
   The strictest reckoning must before Him set :
Then shall the Shepherd fill the fullest fold.
Sad he that when his latest hour is told,
   Hath for his only payment alien sweat,
Since for a money-price his soul he sold !


## CCXXXV.

*Como podes (ó cego Peccador !)*
(A Sermon-sonnet).


How canst (O Sinner blindly gone astray !)
   Prolong thine errors taking scanty tent ;
   Knowing one Moment sees our life-tide spent,
A span comparèd with Eternal Day ?
Deem not the Judge whose justice none gainsay
   Shall spare for sinners torturing punishment
   Nor lapse of Time, albe his steps are lent,
Death-day of horriblest terror shall delay.

Cease then to squander hours, days, months and years
   In seeking friendship with thy foeman, Ill ;
Friendship that greater crop of Evil bears.
   And, since of such deceits thou knowest thy fill,
For Truth now fly these snares of hopes and fears
   And pray His pardon with thy humblest will.

———

## CCXXXVI.

*Verdade, Amor, Razão, Merecimento,*
(A second Sermon-sonnet).

Verity, Amor, Reason, Meritment
  Shall dower with strength and bravery any sprite,
  But Time, Mischances, Fate and Fortune's might
O'er this confusèd world hold regiment.
Thousand Effects in brooding thoughts are pent,
  While Cause remains unknown to human sight:
  But know that more than Life and Death no wight
Can learn by height of man's Intendiment.

Here shall wise Barons high-flown reasons give;
  Yet 'tis Experience 'proves herself most apt:
  And thus much-seeing is the safest test.
Here things may happen wherein none believe:
  And things believèd are that never hapt.
    But CHRIST'S belief is ever bestest best.

## CCXXXVII.

*De Babel sobre os rios nos sentámos,*
(Second Babylonian Sonnet: Cf. Sonn. 194).

On Babylon-waters sunk in woe sat we,
  From our douce Home-land ever banishèd
  With grounded eye and hands on face bespread,
We wept and pining, Zion! remembered thee.
Our Harps we hangèd on the willow-tree,
  Harps that in other day rare musick shed:
  Other the days forsure and other dread;—
Our Harps we quit to quit sad memory.

They, who had carried off the Captive-throng,
Bade us upraise a merry-hearted strain :—
"Sing ye (they say us) hymns of Zion-hill ! "
On such wrong-doing heaped they sorer Ill,
When foes demanded with tyrannick wrong
They sing and carol that would weep and 'plain.

## CCXXXVIII.

*Sobre os rios do Reyno escuro, quando*
(Same subject.   Cf. Redondilhas, I.).

When, on the Rivers where the black Reign lies,
　　Saddened by sorrows for our sins ordainèd,
　　From banisht eyne hot tears in floods we rainèd,
And sighed we, Holy Zion ! for thee our sighs :
They who our souls infested tyrant-wise,
　　And, aye in error, us their thralls enchainèd ;
　　Vainly our psalms and songs to order deignèd,
When all were silent in our miseries.

Upstood we saying :—" Howso chaunt our lay,
　　Canticles grateful to a God benign,
When thus His foemen we perforce obey ? "
　　But now, sole Holy Lord ! 'tis my design,
Leaving of vile extremes the all-vicious way,
　　Henceforth to chaunt the Chaunts of Love Divine.

## CCXXXIX.

*Em Babylonia sobre os rios, quando*
(Same subject).

When by the Rivers Babylon doth rail,
  Thou Holy Zion! we remembered thee,
  There sat we pine-full pains of Thought to dree
And 'parted happiness (hapless!) to bewail.
Leaving the Harps that here of musick fail
  Our hands up-hanged them on strange willow-tree
  When of the songs we sang (Thy psalmody)
Insisting foemen fain would hear the tale.

This wise spake we the squadded hostile throngs :—
  " How can we sing, in homeless land astray,
Our songs to Him, His sacred holy songs ? "
  If I forgot thee best and only stay,
  (My single solace here in sorest wrongs)
*Oblivioni detur dextra mea.*

## CCXL.

*Aponta e bella Aurora, Luz primeira,*
(Immaculate Conception, " quasi Aurora consurgens ").

Breatheth the fair Aurora, primal Sheen
  That brought high tidings of that clearest Day :
  Busk ye and boun ye, Hearts ! in glad array
And welcome Her, Life's Messenger ye ween.
For our Redemption born is a Go-between
  Thy joy, O Heavenly Kingdom ! haste display ;
  Soon shalt thou hallow earth with heavenly sway,
Soon shall from Heaven our fête by Thee be seen.

Marvelleth Nature such pure work to sense ;
　　Shudder with fear confused the Realms infernal,
Seeing Her born exempt fro' Sin's offence.
　　'Twas general Law that ruled thro' Time's Eternal :
But He, the Lord of Law, pure Excellence,
　　For Sanctuary guarded thee, Maternal.

## CCXLI.

*Porque a Terra no Ceo se agasalhasse,*
(The Incarnation.　Cf. Sonn. 299).

That Earth in Heaven mote asylum find
　　God for a Heaven on Earth asylum fand :
　　There not containing, here a place He plann'd,
For He more largeness There from Here design'd.
That by the Godhead rise to God mankind
　　For men the Godhead deigned to be enmann'd :
　　So lowered His height divine to human stand
That mote the human grow to be divine'd.

Look what gave He and what we gave in lieu :
　　Ne'er fade such blessing fro' man's heart memorious:
He gave us boon of life ; His life we slew.
　　He changed for pains of sin His reign all-glorious :
He dealt us Triumphs which to Him were due :—
　　Love was the Doer of such Deed victorious.

———

\*

## CCXLII.

*Que estila a Arvore sacra ? Hum licor santo.*
(The Crucifixion : an Amœbæan).

What drips the Holy Tree ?—" A Saintly tear."
    For whom ?—" For all who be of human strain."
    What use hath it ?—" 'Tis medicine sovereign."
Wherefore?—" For worldly sins and weeping drear."
How may it work ?—" To Luzbel mighty fear."
    Why so ?—" Because his apple bred such bane."
    What bane ?—" With single snare he saw us slain."
Hath it such power ?—" Such power right clear we
    speer."

Who goes up-Cross ?—" He that from Heaven came
    down."                     [invade."
Came down and why?—" That Man high Heaven
What then of Earth would He?—" In Heaven to 'throne."
    Leads there a ladder ? " Yea, securely stay'd."
Who obligèd Him ?—" Victorious Love alone."
    What loved this Maker thus ?—" The thing He
    made."

## CCXLIII.

*Oh ! Arma unicamente só triunfante,*
(Of Dom Sebastiam's Banner ?  Cf. Sonn. 351).

Oh one and only Arm, victorious Vaunt,
    And single Valvarte of the lives of men,
    Whereby our losses gainèd purest gain,
Losses that joyèd Tartarus' horrid haunt !
Follow the Church's Banner militant,
    Which to such holy victories can attain,
    For hosts of spirits, weaned from errors vain,
Here overwander Ponent, there Levant.

O Tree Sublime, with marquetry engrail'd
   Of white and cramoisie and patine'd gold,
With richest rubin crusted and amaill'd
   And deckt with Trophies of a worth untold !
Death to Life dealt in Thee our eyne beheld,
   That Life-in-Death we might thro' Thee behold.


## CCXLIV.

*Aos homẽes hum só Homem pos espanto,*
(Sam Joam Baptista ; venit in testimonium).


One Man man's nature with high marvel prankt,
   Prankt with such marvel for humanity,
   Mortal as man yet Angel-pure was He,
For-that with saintly souls ere born He rankt.
He was a Prophet when in womb enflankt ;
   Amid the highmost high was his degree,
   Who (without seeing) the Great Light could see,
Having for Tromp the Logos Sacrosanct.


He was that Voice, whose loud canorous call
Rang through the concave of the resonant sphere ;
'Twas his the Sinless Body to baptise ;
His Ear the Father's loving Voice could hear ;
He to the subtle question, mystical,     .
Gave gentling answer in sincerest guise.

---

## CCXLV.

*Vós só podeys, sagrado Evangelista,*
(To the discipulus quem diligebat, &c.).

You only, consecrate Evangelist !
   Angel of love-brent Seraph-origin ;
   And in all kenning to the Cherubs kin,
Could be of learnèdest Love the Annalist.
Divine and Kingly Erne ! whose glances wist
   One Who was endless and did ne'er begin ;
   Of Jacob best belovèd Benjamin,
Prower than Joseph in the champion's list.

Apostle-envoy, Prophet, Patriarch ;
   Who from the Prince of Heaven most favour won ;
   And, on His bosom sleeping, most could sight.
You whom the Godhead marked with brother-mark ;
   You of the perfect Mother chosen Son,
   Enjoy the clearest day in flesh and sprite !

## CCXLVI.

*Como louvarey eu, Serafim santo,*
(St. Francis of Assisi).

How shall I, holy Seraph ! hymn the praise
   Of such humility, such penitence ?
   Chastity, Povert, Patience so immense,
In these mine artless, unadornèd lays ?
Theme which the Muses' very choir affrays,
   Dumbing most eloquent grandiloquence.
   O Species dight by Holy Providence
Who Self for weal so great in you displays.

You, of the Saintly Brethren rarest mine,
Sent thousand thousand Souls to heavenly goal
From a lost world you healèd sound and whole ;
You stole not only with your learned line
The wills of mortals, but the Will Divine,
When His five Rubies from His Wounds you stole.


## CCXLVII.

*Ditosas Almas, que ambas juntamente*
(Epitaph on husband and wife.)

Ye happy Spirits ! who at once in twain
   Flew to the sky of Love, the Venus-sky,
   Where Goods enjoyèd here with joys that fly,
Enjoy ye now with joys that e'er remain.
That so contented state ye held so fain,
   Whose brief endurance was its sole annoy,
   Now you have changèd for more joyous joy,
Whose bliss aye waxing ne'er shall wan nor wane.

Sad he that here must live his life begirt
By lover-fineness, by Love's agonies
Whose growth of glory groweth greater grief !
Sad ! for my sufferings ne'er my pains appease ;
And Love has dealt me, for a sorer hurt,
A life so large for Evil so unlief.

## CCXLVIII.

*Contente vivi já, vendome isento*
(Written for a friend ?).

Content I livèd erst, when seeing me free
   From Ills I saw bewailèd by their prey :
   They clepe him Love, I clepe him other way
Discord, Unreason, Warfare, Misery.
The name bewitchèd every Thought of me,
   Who by such name could fail to fare astray ?
   Now am I such, I dread to see the day
When naught of suffering I am doomed to see.

With long despairing and a longing sprite
   He pays the sorrows I for him must brook,
   And e'en mine Evils ill his heart can rest.
Then, on so many Ills I still must sight
   (To deal me thousand more) an angel look,
   And not to heal them an enhardened breast.

## CCXLIX.

*Deixa Apolo o correr tão apressado,*
(Application unknown).

Forego, Apollo, thy so hasty course ;
   Chase not the Nymph whose pride is sans Compare :
   Leads thee not Love, thy leader is a snare
Which brings with shadowed weal woes doubly worse.
And granted Love it were, 'twere love by force :
   And if 'tis forcèd 'twill misfortune bear,
   Then spare a semblance more than mortal fair,
Nor see a treën shape its charms encorse.

Nill thou to forfeit for one vain Content
  The sight that maketh all thy life contented :
In thine own favour moderate thine Intent :
  Less evil 'tis, with her to sight presented,
To dree her coyness and thy pains lament,
  Than feel the loss of her for aye absènted.

## CCL.

*Nas Cidades, nos bosques, nas florestas,*
(To Our Lady of the Martyrs, at Punhete ?).

In bosque and forest, in the mart and meet,
  In vales, on wooded mountain-range thy praise
  Shepherds shall ever sing with tuneful lays,
Thro' coolth of morning, through the noontide-heat.
And in this Temple, where thou dost repeat
  The boons thou dealest in thy blessed ways,
  With Psalm and Hymn and floral Wreaths thy Days
Thy Holy Days mankind ne'er fail to greet !

These offer hands, those feet before thy Fane ;
  Those on thine altars hang a votive store
Of deep-sea monster and the prison chain.
But I my cares, my snares, my ban, my bane,
  (Horrider monsters) and a myriad more,
Bring thee for gifts wi' Longings longed in vain.

## CCLI.

*Vi queixosos de Amor mil namorados,*
(Petrarch : femmina è cosa mobil.   Part I. Sonn. 131).

I saw a thousand lovers Love betwyte,
　None saw I ever give dear Love his due :
　And whoso loudest loves at Love to shrew
I see the latest fro' his cares take flight :
If an Love's dolours do you such despite
　Why thus Love's dolours do you seek and sue?
　And, if Love's dolours you as favours view,
Why are they dolours by you lovers hight ?

Think not to find of joyaunce smallest boon
　In Love, for sadness is his life and law ;
　　In smiling Fortune when her Smiles you see.
In Him and Her I fand the self-same Moon,
　A Moon whose constancy the world ne'er saw
　　Save the consistentest inconstancy.

## CCLII.

*Se lagrimas choradas de verdade*
(Cf. Eclogue V. 10).

If tears in torrents and in truth beshed
　Could soften marble howso dour and dure,
　Why should not mine begot of Love so pure
Quicken a bosom to compassion dead?
For you my freedom, Dame ! I forfeitèd,
　Nor of my proper life I live secure :
　Break of your cruel will the castled mure ;
Nor let your rigour to extremes be sped.

To prize despisal make, in fine, a fine :
None call you Cruel. name to her well due
Who the fon sigh-full lover flouts to shame.
Teach, then, your stony breast some ruth to rue
In what regards you ; 'tis no right of mine :
For I adventure Life—you 'venture name.

## CCLIII.

### *Ja me fundey en vãos contentamentos*
(Autobiographic).

Erst upon vain Contents I based my mind
  When lived I wholly snarèd by the snare
  Of one phantastick Good, of single Care
Cared for by nothing save by Thought struck blind.
Through days and hours and moments I repine'd
  This load of guiling Love's sore weight to bear,
  For I held only him as Fortune's heir
Who for Love only oftest drank the Wind.

But now that true account I come to know,
  I am wholly undeceived of his deceit ;
    For Time gives all things, Time shall all discoure.
Least shall the fullest Love his brim o'erflow ;
  His joys are richest (this I ne'er did weet)
    Whoso of Love-wealth lives the poorest poor.

————

## CCLIV.

*Em huma lapa, toda tenebrosa,*
(A Scherzo : written for a friend ?).

Deep in a cavern gloomed with gathered night,
   Where beat the billows raging wild and wood,
   With hand supporting cheek (as saw I) stood
A Nymph of gentlest mien in care-full plight :
As black in mourning as in beauty bright,
   Her eyne distillèd seed o'pearl in flood ;
   And briny ocean stayed his boisterous mood
A thing so sightly and so woe to sight.

At whiles she viewed the horrid steepy Head
   With her soft eyne, whose glance of sweetest lure
     Sufficed his stony core with care to melt.
And in her angel-voice at length she said :—
   " Ah me, how oft they most lack Aventùre
     To whom Dame Nature most of merit dealt."

## CCLV.

*Se em mim (ó Alma) vive maes lembrança*
(Sufistical).

If in me other memory live, O Sprite !
   Of aught beyond my boast of lo'ing you,
   Lost be the joys I 'joy when viewing you
And lose I even Hope to see your sight.
Be seen in me so coy and rustick wight
   That undeserves to boast of knowing you ;
   May the more good I would be doing you
Only offend you if I change my plight.

I stand confirmèd and this fact maintain ;
  By your most cruel will my love be weigh'd ;
On me your harshness prove its hard disdain.
  A Truth so truthful I to heart have laid
Sithence in plighted troth of purest strain
  What Will I had your tributary I made.


## CCLVI.

*Ilustre Gracia, nombre de una moça.*
(Spanish : Parody of Garcilasso : Sonn. 24).

Illustrious Gràcia ! name of Spinster known,
  First-come of witches, and alike in case
  To Mondoñedo, Palma, limping Thrasse,
The magick mitre ever digne to don.
If in the middle of the Church have shown
  The veil (down-falling) your all-shameless face,
  Of you shall clamour all men, high and base,
" See how the Devil wantoneth with his own ! "

She moveth mountains fro' their 'stablished stead ;
  Her words the courses of the tides command ;
    Her spells through sea-waves drive a dry foot-
    way.
Blusheth her birthplace and rich Tage runs red,
  Who for her beareth more of man than sand,
    So shall large tribute some to Hell defray.

———

## CCLVII.

*Qual tem a borboleta por costume,*
(The Poet and the Moth).

Even as Nature's ure the Night-moth dooms,
　Allured and spell-bound by the taper's light,
　To wheel in thousand gyres until her flight
Now in cremation ends, now self consumes :
So run I to the ray my Soul illumes,
　Fired, fair Aonia ! by this eyën-light
　And burn me, howsoe'er my cautious sprite
To free the rational part of me presumes.

I know man's Sight for a daring visionist ;
　How high the human Thought will soar and strain ;
　And how my life to death I surely gave.
But Amor wills not any him resist,
　Nor my soul wills it, which in torment-pain
　E'en as in greater gloire is glad to live.

## CCLVIII.

*Lembranças de meu bem, doces lembranças,*
(Written by Martim de Crasto?).

Memories of happiness mine ! douce Memories
　That aye so lively in my Soul remain,
　Crave ye no more of me, for all the gain
I gained you see how Change has made her prize.
Ay blindfold Love ! Ay Hope's dead vanities
　That could in other days my strength sustain !
　Now shall you leave him who endured your pain
And every trust shall fly with Life that flies.

Yea, trust shall fly with Life, since Aventùre
   Stole in one moment all that Boast so glorious
Which, grown to greatest growth, shall least endure.
   Oh! would Remembrance fleet with joys memorious,
At least my spirit mote abide secure
   With her to win a victory more victorious.


## CCLIX.

*Fermosos olhos, que cuidado days*
(Carpe diem. Cf. Garcilasso : Sonn. 5).

Beautiful eyes which deal an envious care
   To very light of Sunshine purest pure !
   That Sol's all-fairest sheeniest formosure
You leave surpast with splendour sans Compare.
If an ye flout (for that ye shine so fair)
   Love's fineness, ever lief your heart to 'lure,
   See now, sith much you see, may not endure
Your charms resplendent as you would they were.

Pluck, pluck of fleet-foot Time, the fugitive,
   And of your beauty, fairest doucest fruit
   In vain desirèd ere full-ripe it grew.
To me, who die for you, for you who live,
   Make Love pay tribute due to loving suit,
   Happy to pay the tax was due to you.

———

## CCLX.

*Pues siempre sin cessar, mis ojos tristes,*
(Spanish : to a dame who sent him a tear 'twixt two plates).

My lamentable Eyne ! when aye ye wone
   Tearfully treating night and treating day,
   See an be this true Tear that doth convey
That Sun which oft tide made you shed your own.
If you assure me that your sight have shown
   The Tear a Tear, 'twill be my sort and stay ;
   And, from this hour, I'll hold in wisest way
Were shed the many shed for her alone.

But whatsoever thing much coveted,
   Tho' we behold it, fails our faith to gain ;
Much less this mister thing ne'er 'maginèd.
   Still I assure you, though the Tear you feign,
Enough the Tear to me for Tear you sped
   That I this Tear for Tear shall e'er maintain.

## CCLXI.

*Tem feito os olhos neste apartamento*
(By Pedro da Cunha ?).

Have shed these eyelids, in this banishment,
   Of after-yearnings a tempestuous sea,
   Which added pining to the pine of me
And upon sentiment heaped sentiment.
My sufferings turn to pangs which aye torment,
   Pity is turned to pitiless penalty ;
   And so is Reason wrecked by Will that she
Enslaves to Evil mine intendiment.

Tongue ne'er attaineth what the Soul can sense ;
  And so, if any wish at any hour
    To ken what bin uncomprehended Grief,
Leave he his lover, and experience
  That before parting I had lesser stowre
    To part from living better to have Life.

## CCLXII.

*A Peregrinaçao de hum pensamento*
(By Martim de Crasto ?).

The Pilgrimaging of a Thought intent,
  Which of mine Ill makes habit and costume,
  Doth of my sorry life so much consume,
As grow the causes that my soul torment.
By grief of suffering sufferance goeth spent ;
  But so is spent my Soul no lights illume,
  That wrapt in Weal whereto she dares presume,
Of Evils hent in hand she takes no tent.

Afar I feared (as though could Fear protect)
  What dangers drumming at the door I see,
  When in me nothing find I safe or sure.
But now I reck (O never had I reckt !)
  That man's poor wits in Love's captivity,
    Save cure of Fortune ne'er shall know a cure.

## CCLXIII.

*Achome da Fortuna salteado,*
(By Martim de Crasto?).

I find me waylaid by that bandit Fate ;
  Time fleeth flitting with his fleetest flight,
  Leaving me doubtful of my life's own light
And every moment driven more desperate.
To Care so care-full changed my careless State ;
  Where gloire is greatest groweth grisliest blight :
  Nor live I fearing loss with aught affright,
Nor for regain of me in trust I wait.

Whatever bird abide in wildest hill,
  Whatever bestial in his lair repose,
    All have glad hours ; mine all are sad with spleen.
You, Eyne ! aye pining by your proper will
  (For Love defrays me with his torment-woes)
    Weep when you see the scene your sight hath
      seen.

## CCLXIV.

*Se no que tenho dito vos offendo,*
(F. y S. ends.  By Dr. Alvaro Vaz?).

If aught I haply said your heart offend,
  'Twas no desire of mine in aught to offend you ;
  For though my merits ne'er pretence pretend you,
Ne'er to dismerit you will I pretend.
But sure my Fate is such (as I intend),
  Whate'er I gainèd striving to intend you,
  Hereto hath never made me comprehend you,
For I my proper self misapprehend.

The Days, with aidance lent by Aventùre,
  Each man and every from illusion wean ;
While misadventure undeceives no fewer.
  Which better serves me may declare my teen
Or joys I erst enjoyèd, while endure
  This life so large that years so few hath seen.

---

# PART II.

## (Nos. 265–301).

## CCLXV.

*Doce contentamento já passado,*
(Autobiographic).

Sweetest Content that was with joys that were,
  Wherein consisted all the Weal I knew ;
  Who thus your dear companionship withdrew
And left me lonesome far fro' you to fare ?
Who reckt to see him in this state of care
  While those brief hours by joyaunce featherèd flew,
  When giglet Fortune gave consent I view ·
My cares full feeding upon sleight and snare ?

My Fortune 'proved her coy and cruel elf,
  She caused my losses, she and only she
    From whom all caution were but wasted pains.
Nor let created thing deceive itself,
  No sort prevention man shall ever free
    To fly those evils which his star ordains.

## CCLXVI.

*Sempre, cruel Senhora, receei,*
(Complaining of infidelity).

Ever, my cruel Faire ! with fear I strave,
    Your un-trust viewing with a meting glance,
    Lest grow to' Unlove your tardy dalliance ;
Lest, since I love you, self I fail to save.
Perish, in fine, whate'er Hope bade me crave,
    Since you on other love build esperance :
    Now shall so puissant be your change and chance
As ever hid I what to you I gave.

I gave you life and sent ; I gave my sprite ;
    O'er all this *me* I gave you lordship-power ;
        You promise love and promised love deny.
Now am I suchwise, so forlorn of plight,
    I ken not whither wend I, but some hour
        Heavy on you shall this remembrance lie.

## CCLXVII.

*Fortuna em mim guardando seu direito*
(Autobiographic).

Fortune o'er me reserving rightful Hest
    In green my Joyaunce joyed to cast away.
    O how much Happiness ended on that day
Whose sad Remembrance burneth in my breast !
All contemplating, my suspicion guess'd
    For Weal so pleasant this surcease must pay
    Lest every worldling say and truly say
That world-deceits can breed of Weals the best.

But an my Fortune (to discount me bent)
  Dealt me such Blessing and such Sentiment lent me
Of Memory, only to destroy me lent ;
  How then can blame me Suffering this wise sent me,
If the same cause it useth to torment,
  I hold best cause to bear what Ills torment me ?


## CCLXVIII.

*Se a Fortuna inquieta, e mal olhada,*
(Answer to one who praised him).


If aye-unquiet Fortune evil-eyed,
  Loving the justest laws of Heaven to infame,
  That quiet life, which doth her Unlove claim,
Would grant me, 'joying honest restful tide :
Haply my Muse by happiness glorified
  In light more ardent, in a livelier flame,
  Our Tagus bedded in his patrial frame
With lilt of lyre beloved had lullaby'd :

But since my Destiny, dealing toil and moil
That dark my weakling Muse so weary faring,
Doth to such high-toned praise deny consent ;
Then let your Muse, of generous laud unsparing,
Seek other subject of a higher coil,
And to the admiring World yourself present.

## CCLXIX.

*Este amor que vos tenho limpo, e puro,*
("Worth half The Lusiads," said Bocage).

This Love for you I keep so chaste and pure,
  No touch of villein purpose can abate,
  Dating from tenderest age his earliest date,
I strive this only in this soul endure.
That it shall nowise change I wone secure,
  Sans fear of any freak or false of Fate,
  Or Good supremely good, or sorriest state,
Or Present safe, or Future aye unsure.

Fast fades the Daisy and the flowers go die,
  Winter and Summer strew them all a-field,
  For my love only 'tis eternal May :
But, Ladye ! seeing you every grace deny,
  And seeing your thankless heart no favour yield,
  My love misleads me lost in sore dismay.

## CCLXX.

*Se grande gloria me vem só de olhar-te,*
(Variant of No. 148).

If be my greatest glory but to view thee,
  'Tis grief unequal when my sight forlore thee ;
  If by my merits I presume implore thee,
Full dear I pay the false desires that sue thee :
If as thou art with praises I approve thee,
  I know that I, as I, offend before thee.
  If ill I will me for-that I adore thee,
What prize can seek I higher than to love thee ?

Extremes of love-pains these I bear so woe,
  Ah my sweet glory ! Ah my threasury !
And when I deem them gone again they grow.
  This wise my Memory holds one only Thee ;
I n'ote an I be live or dead, I know
  That Battle's properest end be Victory.


## CCLXXI.

*A formosura desta fresca serra,*
(Of Cintra, or perhaps of Ceuta).


These Mountain-beauties of the freshest green,
  These verdant chestnuts shedding shadows chill ;
  The unhurried rail of many a murmurous rill,
Banishing sorrow from the gladding scene :
Hoarse Ocean-whispers ; regions strange, seldseen ;
  Sol slowly westering 'neath the horizon-hill ;
  The clustering flocks and herds that linger still,
Cloud-armies battling in the blue Serene :

In fine, whatever rarest fairest Nature
Offers with prodigal show of varied store,
Dealeth me (thee unseen) but sore unweal :
Sans thee all 'noyeth me who all abhor ;
Sans thee I feel and shall for ever feel
In greatest gladness sadness even greater.

## CCLXXII.

*Sospechas, que en mi triste phantasia*
(Spanish : by Garcilasso ?).

Doubts that my dolorous phantasies affright !
　Still on my senses warfare ye declare,
　Stirring, re-stirring in this breast my care,
And mar with cruel hand my day, my night :
Now my Resistance hath forlore his might ;
　Now doth my Spirit her defence forbear :
　I own you victor, and repenting fare
I ever fought you with such obstinate fight.

Then bear me sudden to that awesome stead
Where not to see my doom ensculptured shown,
Hereto mine eyelids strove I closed to keep.
Now I ground weapons, for to hold his own
And hold so hard, the World a wretch forbade :
Then all my spoilings on your charet heap !

## CCLXXIII.

*Sustenta meu viver huma esperança*
(Suspecting infidelity).

Only one single Hope my life sustaineth
　Derived fro' single Good I so desire,
　For when it plighteth me a troth entire
My greatest doubt fro' smallest change obtaineth :
And when this Welfare highest place attaineth,
　Raising my raptured Soul to height still higher,
　To see *him* win such Weal inflames my ire
For-that his Sovenance place for you disdaineth.

Thus in this net-work so enmeshed I wone,
  My life I hardly give, for aye sustenting
A novel matter heapt on cares I own.
  Sighings of sadness from my bosom venting,
Musick'd by whizzing shot of cannon-stone,
  I fare, these wretched matters still lamenting.

## CCLXXIV.

*Já nað sinto, Senhora, os desenganos,*
(Another complaint of infidelity).

No more, Madàme! feel I false hopes and fears
  Wherewith your coying aye my fondness tried,
  Nor sight I guerdon to my love denied,
Guerdon deservèd by the faith of years.
Lone I my loss beweep, lone shed my tears,
  When seeing, Ladye! who my place supplied:
  But here you single-handed 'venged my pride
On your ungrateful sprite, your snares, your fleers

Gives double glory whatso vengeänce
  The Wight offended taketh on the Offender,
  When satisfaction comes in righteous way:
But now your coyness, your ill change and chance
  I see their vengeance-debt so fully render,
  E'en I pray never so high price you pay.

———

## CCLXXV.

*Que póde já fazer minha Ventura,*
(A Complaint: autobiographic).

What now can Fortune to my lot secure
   That shall have power with joy my life to grace?
   Or how foundations of my Future base
On baseless visions evermore unsure?
What pain so certain, or what pang so dure,
   That can be greater than my gruesome case?
   How shall to any fear my Thought give place
If all mine evils but my Thoughts depure?

Like one who learneth in his youth the craft
   Of eating Poisons blent with cunning skill, ✔
     Whose ancient usance breeds immunity:
Thus I, accustomed to the venom-draught,
   And used to sufferance of my present ill,
     Feel naught of feeling for futurity.

## CCLXXVI.

*Quando cuido no tempo, que contente*
(Sufistical).

As I o'ermuse times passèd, when content
   I saw the seed-of-pearl, snow, rose and gold,
   Like one who seeth vision'd Wealth untold,
Meseems the Present doth my Past present;
But, in the passing of such Accident,
   When I so far fro' you my death behold,
   I fear lest every Thought ill-bode unfold,
I fear lest Fancy fain herself absent:

The days are many since by aventùre
  I saw you, Ladye! (an so dare I say)
    With eyne of heart that naught of fear could see.
Now in so hapless case am I unsure
  E'en of my Fancy and your 'noyous way :
    This bin a riddle I may never ree.


## CCLXXVII.

*Quando, Senhora, quiz amor qu' amasse*
(Written for a friend?).


When Love, my Ladye! willèd that I love
  This great perfection and this gentle gree,
    He straight gave sentence that the cruelty
Which fills your bosom growth of love should prove.
He willèd nothing me fro' you remove,
  Ne dure disfavour ne asperity ;
    But on my spirit rare in constancy
Your cruel coyness work its will behoove.

And sithence here you see me offering you
  This your own Spirit for your sacrifice,
    Cease, cease to glut your greed of cruel Will.
Deem not, my Ladye! larger life my due,
  These ceasing Days shall die with one device,
    My faith defending, true and loyal still.

———

## CCLXXVIII.

*Eu vivia de lagrimas isento,*
(Autobiographic).

Exempt fro' tears I wended life-tide's way,
   In one delightful and deceivèd creed ;
   However richer another amourist's meed,
A thousand glories for one pang ne'er pay.
Seeing mine inner man such thoughts obey,
   No Wealth an envious wish in me could breed ;
   Lively I livèd, had of dread no heed,
With doucest sentiment, Love's doucest fay.

Greedy was Fortune ; straightway she bereft
My life of lightsome, glad, contented lot,
And, as it never were, Weal turned to stowre :
In change of which my Welfare here she left
Memories that do me dead at every hour,
Bringing to memory Weals that now are not.

## CCLXXIX.

*Indo o triste Pastor todo embebido*
(Subject unknown).

The tristful Shepherd dolour-drowned would hie
   In shadowy visions of the sweetest Sent,
   And to the legier windlets made lament,
The while his spirit sighed its softest sigh :
" To whom complain me, lost and blinded I,
   For sticks and stones discoure no sentiment ?
   Whom speak ? On whom my tale of torment vent ?
Where call I loudest least is heard my cry !

" O lovely Nymph ? Why deign thou not respond ?
Why hold so precious e'en a glance, a sight ?
    Why cause my querele ever 'plain my woe ?
" The more I seek thee more thou dost abscond !
The worse thou seest me harder sets thy sprite !
    Thus with mine Evil must its Causes grow."

## CCLXXX.

*De hum taõ felice engenho, produzido*
(Elegiacs to D. Simam da Silveira).

That happy genius thine, begot and grown
    By other, clearest Sol saw naught more bright,
It suits to nourish mind wi' Thoughts high-flown
    All digne of praises, all with marvel dight.
A long-gone writer was Musæus hight,
    A Sage and Poet allwheres man-beknown,
Taught by the Lover of the tuneful Sprite
    Who made Infernals hang his tones upon.

His lay the mute-surd mountain-range could shake,
    Singing that Ill whereof felt I the sting,
The Abydos Youngling by his wits forsake :
    Now tell the self-same tale (I hear them sing)
Tasso and our Boscam, who both outspake
    The blinding movements of the bisson King.

## CCLXXXI.

*Dizei, Senhora, da belleza idéa ;*
(Half-satirical : Petrarch, Part I. Sonnet 30).

Beauty's ideal, Ladye ! deign me say
　For weaving tresses of that aureate shine
　Where yode you finding gold refined so fine,
Fro' what dark mine or vein of precious ley ?
Those eyne how robbed they such Phœbèan ray ?
　Whence this grave gracious favour, empery-digne ;
　Or did you win them by the Lere Divine
Or haply used Medea's gramarye ?

Fro' what sea-wombèd shell did you select
　The pearls of precious Oriental beam,
　　Shown in sweet laughing smiles that bliss and
　　　bless us ?
Since you enform'd you as you did elect,
　Mount guard on self; shun see your sight a-stream,
　Fly every fountain : Ne'er forget Narcissus.

## CCLXXXII.

*Na ribeira do Euphrates assentado,*
(Ecce iterum Babylonia !)

I sat me lonesome on Euphrates-shore,
　And fand me talking things of memory,
　Of that brief blessing and that high degree
In thee, sweet Zion ! I had known of yore.
Asking the causes of my state forlore
　Quoth they :—" Why singst thou not the history
　Of weal that went, of that supremacy
Which o'er all Evils made thee Conqueror ?

" Knowst not man lulleth by the sound of song
   Woes howsoever dire and rigorous-dure ?
     Sing then, nor weeping thus expend thy breath ! "
Sighing I answered, " Whenas wax so strong
   Man's after-yearnings, Pity cannot cure
     By voice of singing : Pity deals us death."

## CCLXXXIII.

*El vaso relusiente, y crystalino,*
(Spanish : on a present of perfume : not by Camoens?).

That Vial lucident and chrystalline,
   " Angeles-water," limpid, odorous,
     Enwrapt in silkiest silk, and rosiest rose
And bound with tresses from the golden mine :
Right plain appearèd it some Gift divine,
   Wrought by the Art most artful art endows
     Of that blanch Nymph, whose grace more gracious
       shows
Than ruby blushing in the Morn's sunshine :

This Vial your body figureth to the viewer,
   Enstreaked by members of the fairest fair
And in its Perfume breathes your spirit pure ;
   The silk your blanchness showeth, and the hair
Makes binding fetters ; such the ligature
   That chained my Freedom with so facile snare.

## CCLXXXIV.

*Chorai Nymphas, os fados poderosos*
(The subject unknown).

Bewail, ye Nymphs ! the fiat of fatal might
　Which could that sovran loveliness bewray.
　Say whither farèd (to the tomb a prey)
Those Eyne so gracious lit with royal light ?
O worldly welfare, snare-fraught, strong of sleight !
　What grief to hear that such all-lovely May
　Lies reft of splendour in the Grave's dure clay—
Such face of beauty, locks so wonder-bright !

What shall to others hap, since Death had power
Over a Being of such shine and sheen
Eclipsing clearest rays of brightest day !
But ne'er deservèd her this mundane scene,
Wherefore she deignèd stay on Earth no more,
And to her home (the Heavens) she winged her way.

## CCLXXXV.

*Senhora já desta alma, perdoai*
(Written for a friend ?).

Ladye my Spirit's now liege lord ! condone
　Of one Love-conquered madness-pain and pine,
　And with those eyes bestow one glance benign
On this pure passion by my Spirit shown.
On my pure faith (naught else) your glance be thrown,
　See of mine extreme woes the subtle sign ;
　And if of any pain you deem them digne,
Avenge you, Ladye mine ! on me alone.

Let not the grief that burns my grief-full breast
  Cause pain and sorrow aye my bosom tear—
The heart Love vassal'd e'er to do your hest.
  Restrain you, Ladye ! lest some few declare
That in so beauteous object, rarely blest,
  Ingratitude to dight her dwelling dare.


## CCLXXXVI.

*Quem vos levou de mim, saudoso estado,*
(Written for a friend ?).


Who fro' me robbèd you, O wistful State !
  Which on my Reason such Unreasons tried ?
  Who was't for whom I was so soon denied,
Forgetting all the Weal whilòm so great ?
You changed my resting for unresting fate,
  And in its cruel harshness bade me 'bide ;
  You have denayed me faith to me affied,
When to your truth I gave the most of weight.

I lived withouten fear of aught so woe ;
  Fortune, who dealeth all by her decree,
    Unlove for love returned me to my cost.
That naught availeth this my case I know,
  Man is born wailing—'tis but just that he
    Pay with his wailing what he loved and lost.

## CCLXXXVII.

*Diversos casos, varios pensamentos*
(Petrarch, I. 14).

Differing cases, Thought of varied sents
  So bring confusèd mine Intendiment,
  That now in nothing see I least Content,
Save when Contentments end in Miscontents.
In various cases, various sentiments
  Befall, for showing to our sentiment
  Man's aspirations are but windy vent
When rest he painteth based on vain intents.

That long discourses breed Desire we see,
  When comes Occasion time and tide deranging,
And care unrecks Impossibility :
Th' unjust one standeth where the just should be ;
  We view hard hills their fixt foundations changing ;
I, only I, unchangèd dule must dree.

## CCLXXXVIII.

*Doce sonho, suave, e soberano,*
(Traum—Schaum. Cf. Boscam, 61).

Sweet Dream of joyaunce suavest, sovereign,
  Would for a longer time it lasted me !
  Ah, had no waking spoilt my dreamery,
Such disillusion, such ungain to gain !
Ah Good delicious ! Ah douce snaring bane !
  Could I for larger space its trickery see,
  If then my life had fled her misery,
For pride and pleasure I to die were fain.

Happy was I-not-I when visions showed
  The Weal I hoped to see with broad-wake eyes.
  Look ye what payment doth fro' Fate befall !
In fine when I-not-I such blessing owed,
  There was some reason for my luck in Lies,
    Since in the things of Truth my luck was small.


## CCLXXXIX.

*Diana prateada, esclarecida*
(Of the type jocose).

Dian enlightenèd with silvern light,
  The light hot Phœbus to his sister lent,
  Being of very nature lucident,
Shone forth her radiance as in mirror pight.
Ten myriad million graces deckt her sight,
  When to mine eyes appeared that excellent
  Ray of your proper semblance, different
In grace and love fro' what before was dight.

Such full of favours I a-sudden seeing
  And eke, so near to being all your own,
    Lauded the moonlit hours, night's clear-obscure :
By night you dealt my Love his very being,
  Wherefore I gather clear, by night alone
    And ne'er by day-light is my luck secure.

## CCXC.

*A lá en Monte Rei, en Bal de Laça,*
(In Gallego dialect : to Violante, spinning).

There on the Monte Rey, in Val de Lace,
  I saw Biolante by a river-bed,
  So sweet a seeing 'twas, I chilled with dread
When seen in mortal gear immortal grace :
From long fair distaff drew my Shepherdess
  The silken thread a-spinning, when I said,
  " Behold me dying, shear my life-tide's thread ! "
Quoth she, " I shear it not, pass safe apace ! "

" How pass apace when here I'd wone in stead ?
  And if I pass (quoth I) 'tis danger pure ;
For without spirit bides a body dead."
  " By this my life thou robbest ! rest thou sure
Thou die not Shepherd !"—" Shepherdess I dread ;
  Meseems my biding be the more secure."

## CCXCI.

*Porque me faz, amor, inda acá torto,*
(Gallego : to the same).

Why, Love ! here, even here, so work my bane ?
  Betide thee, shameless god, a doom as dread !
  Low carlish lad, a guide that so misled
To see Biolante who my life has slain.
I saw her, never to see hythe again,
  Nor find me (hapless I !) a resting stead
  The floods of sorrow at the Ford I shed
Shall prove its comfort when as lacketh rain.

Right well thy Cyprian Mother to my sight
   A pitiful Mundane shows, sans honesty ;
   Sans-loy, false-hearted, cruel, tyrannous Wight :
For, were she other than this self-same She
A kindness so unkind thou ne'er hadst dight,
   Nor she such cruel beast had been for me.


## CCXCII.

*Em quanto Phebo os montes accendia*
(Classical).

While Phœbus flamed the fells with rosy ray
   And fro' mid-Heaven rainèd cloudless light,
   To 'fend her maiden flower fro' bane and blight,
Delia in chasing passed the live-long day.
Venus, sly threading firmamental way
   To win Anchises' will in loving fight,
   Seeing Diana's honest, modest plight
By way of jeering this wise said her say :—

" Thou with thy net-work seekst the coverture
   Fugitive roebucks meshing in thy toil ;
   My toils man's very senses captivate ! "
" Twere better " (gave reply the goddess pure)
   In these my meshes legier bucks to encoil
   Than thou therein be netted by thy mate ! "

## CCXCIII.

*Se de vosso formoso, e lindo gesto*
(Abounds in Variants).

If from your fairy form and graceful geste
    Bloomed pretty blossoms to delight man's eye-sight,
    Which for man's bosom be the durest eye-blight,
In me stands provèd clear and manifest :
Seeing with pudency your beauties drest,
    I saw a thousand posies deckt with Eye-bright ;
    But had my heart worn glasses which man's eye light
I ne'er had seen you deal such wound funest.

An Ill weal-showing, Weal that evil seems
    My thought are raising high o'er human plane
    In thousand several shades of phantasy :
Wherein I ever fare, and fare in dreams,
    While you care nothing save to see my pain,
    That lends foundation to your jubilee.

## CCXCIV.

*N'hum taõ alto lugar de tanto preço*
("Man's Life is honoured by a noble Death." Petrarch, I.
Canz. 16).

Upon so noble height, man's highest prize,
    My will and wishes 'stablishèd I see,
    That e'en Desire there fainteth, for-that she
One all unworthy of such worth espies.
When such low-standing mine I recognize,
    I find my Care extreme immodesty ;
    To die for it were insufficiency
And greater guerdon than my worth affies.

The more than natural claim to high desart
  Of one who causeth me so dreadful doom
    Maketh it every hour grow more and more, ah !
But from far-ranging thoughts I nill depart ;
  For, though this Evil drive me to the tomb,
  *Un bel morir tutta la vita honora.*


## CCXCV.

*Quantas penas, amor, quantos cuidados,*
(By Diogo Bernardes ?).


How many miseries, Love ! what banes inbred
  How many a bootless rain of tearful brine,
  Wherewith a thousand times breast, face and eyne
Are bathed (blind godhead !) for thy sake beshed !
How many mortal sobs and sighs dispread
  From heart so subject to that will of thine !
  As many Ills as thou hast worked, in fine,
All fand employment showering on my head.

Satisfied all things (this I own to thee)
One single eye-glance, love and pity showing
From one who captured me by Fate's command.
O ever blessèd hour such bliss bestowing !
What Fear remains me since 'twas mine to see,
With so much joyaunce mine, a sight so bland ?

## CCXCVI.

*O tempo acaba, o anno, o mez, e a hora,*
(Cf. Sonn. 316).

Time endeth every time, year, month and hour ;
    And force, and art, and wit, and hero-will :
    Time endeth Fame and voideth golden Fill,
And Time Time's being must himself deplore.
Time finds and finishes for evermore
    The force of thankless and enhardened Ill ;
    But Time my surging sorrows ne'er shall still
Until, my Ladye ! you my rest restore.

Time turneth clearest Day to Night obscure,
    Time turneth joyous laugh to tears most triste,
    Time turneth stormiest sea to stillest Main.
But Time ne'er softeneth (of this truth I'm sure)
    That heart, as adamant hard, wherein consist
    Of this my Hope the pleasure and the pain.

## CCXCVII.

*Posto me tem Fortuna em tal estado,*
(Written late in life ?).

Fortune hath placed me in so parlous state
    And so she humbles me her feet before,
    That (lost) for losing own I nothing more,
That (changed) no changing I can now await.
For me all Good is finishèd by Fate,
    Henceforth I find my life as lived forlore ;
    For where such Ill is conned the wide world o'er,
Life shall excuse me living longer rate.

If Will avail me aught I will but die,
    For well becomes me ne'er another Hope,
      And thus I'll cure one Ill with other Ill :
And when so little Weal of Weal hope I,
    Now that one remedy with this Ill can cope,
      To seek such remedy blame they not my Will.


## CCXCVIII.

*Já naõ fere o Amor com arco forte,*
(To Feliza, by candlelight).


No more with force-full bow fares Love to smite,
    Now bin his arrows dasht upon the plain,
      No more (as wont) battayle would he darraign,
The fight he offereth is another fight.
He does us die with eyne through eyën-light
    And, to make sicker Shot ne'er shot in vain,
      Your eyes he choosèd which inorbed contain
More charms than all 'twixt North and South are pight.

Love such almighty power to you hath lent
To live exempt fro' his and fancy-free
(Now while I rhyme the taper's light is spent).
Then if, Feliza ! malcontent you see
My sonnet, pray'e take no further tent
For all is vision shown by Phantasy.

## CCXCIX.

*Pues, lagrimas, tratais mis ojos tristes,*
(Spanish : same subject as Sonn. 260).

Since, Tears ! my tristful eyes ye treat so bold,
   That spend in shedding Tear-flood night and day,
   Look ye if this be Tear she doth convey
For whom so many a rill whilòme ye roll'd :
Perpend, mine Eyes ! what 'tis you here behold
   And if a Tear, O luck to me for aye !
   You have employèd, in the bestest way
For this one single, thousand million-fold.

But whatsoever holds he dearest dear
   (Albe securèd) man will ne'er believe,
Much more the boon that doth unhoped appear.
   Nathless I say you, though the gift deceive,    ·
Enough the Tear be given as a Tear,
   That I as very Tear the Tear receive.

## CCC.

*Olhos formosos em quem quiz natura*
(Cf. Sonns. 38 and 152).

Beautiful Eyes ! which potent Nature bade
   Display her powers in highest, surest sign,
   If ye your pith and puissance would divine,
Look on the Creature you (the Maker) made.
In me your portraiture is clear pourtray'd,
   In all I suffer you are drawn to line :
   For if unequal pains to pass be mine,
Far greater potency your charms display'd.

For self I only crave the Crave of me :
   Yours and yours only I myself esteem,
      That on my head your pledge shall set its seal.
Self I remember not when you I see
   Nor yet the world ; nor err I, for I deem
      That in your Sovenance dwells my worldly Weal.


## CCCI.

*Quem presumir, Senhora, de louvar-vos,*
(Variant of No. 106 : last of Common Editions).


Whoso presumeth, Ladye mine ! to praise you,
   With lore of mortal, not with lere divine,
      He shall be provèd of such Fault condign
As you prove perfect to what sight surveys you.
Let none with praises vain pretend to upraise you,
   However rare his praise and peregrine ;
      So doth your Beauty in my fancy shine
Save with yourself Compare the Lord denays you.

Blest my-your Spirit, which you did embrave
   To take possession of a prize so splendid
As that, my Ladye ! which to me you gave.
   Better than very life I will defend it ;
For, since so tender mercy crowned my Crave,
   In unforgetful memory I will hend it.

*Lyricks*
       Q

# PART III.

(Nos. 302–360).

## CCCII.

*Los que bivis subjectos a la estrela*
(Spanish : apparently pröemium to fourth century).

Ye who live subject to the Venus star,
　And to her lovely Son whom Love we name,
　I speak not those who seeing any dame
Declare her favours life can make or mar :
No ! 'tis to those Love's spark o' life shall gar
　For one and only one wear breast a-flame ;
　And 'mid them only those who burn to claim
The pangs that causes of more loving are :—

Speed you to see my song, where picturèd
　You shall view sundry feats Fate gendereth,
Which in the bowels of my Being are bred :
　Shall see Love's terrible power all perileth :
Shall see his anguish, grame and anxious dread ;
　Sighs, singults, weeping, ugly pains and Death.

## CCCIII.

*Todas as almas tristes se mostravão*
(Repeats Sonns. 41 and 77).

Showed all men's spirits, by their woe down-weigh'd,
　A pious pity for their Lord Divine,
　And, in the presence of His mien benign,
Tribute of praises due to Him they paid :

My free-born senses then my Will obey'd,
  For hereto Destiny held to her design ;
  When eyes, those eyes, whereof I ne'er was digne,
By robbing Reason all my me waylaid.

The bright new Vision struck me stony blind,
  Born of uncustom was the strangest sense
    Of that sweet presence, that angelick air.
To heal my hurt can I no medicine find ?
  Ah ! why did Fortune breed such difference
    Amid the many woman-borns she bare ?

## CCCIV.

*Senhora minha, se de pura inveja*
(Scherzando : to a high-coloured Dame).

My Dame ! if Love of purest jealousy
  Suffer no more that dainty sight be shown,
  That flush of roses on the snow-bed sown,
Those eyes whose shine Sol covets enviously :
He may not rob me so I never see
  Souled in my Soul the charms he made your own,
  Where I will ever make your portrait wone
Nor care how cruel enemy be he :

In sprite I see you, and I view ne'er born
  On plain or prairie, howso fresh and fair,
    Aught save the flower that scenteth every hill :
I see on either cheek red lilies' hue :
  Happy who sees them, but far happier
    Who has and holds them an Earth hold such Weal !

## CCCV.

*Contas, que traz Amor com meus cuidados,*
(Cf. Canz. VI. 7).

Accounts that Cupid keeps with my unhele
  Bid me recount my tale of bitter pain :
  These bin Accounts where thought shall ever strain
Sad pine recounting, Fortune's dire unweal :
Cruel the Accounts would be, if counted ill
  Be all my services, whose end is fain
  To prove of some Account in compt of gain
Themselves accounting Fortune's favourites still.

If haply faring forth your sight I see ;
  Uncounted beading tears ! a torrent turgid,
Caus̀ed by this effect, go, shameless flow !
  There say you be salt drops, for ever surg̀ed
From infinite Ocean, the desire of me,
  That fires the furnace where ye (Tears !) are forg̀ed.

## CCCVI.

*Fermosa mão que o coração me aperta,*
(Probably by Camoens).

That fair-formed Hand my heart in holding takes,
  If my subjected Will it make submit,
  And show such sweetness albe counterfeit,
When shall I see the certainty it makes ?
My slumbers dream-full are, my grief awakes ;
  Complete the pain, the gloire is incomplete ;
  What boots if I asleep the vision greet
Which my awaking eye-glance aye forsakes ?

Love wills my Welfare but his wiles be bold,
  Some good he showeth trickt with cunning skill,
Good that witholdeth most but hath no hold :
  For, when fro' Love-snare I unsnare my will
(Those Ills awaking which a slumber dole'd)
He deals with banisht Weal redoubled Ill.

## CCCVII.

*De tantas perfeiçoens a natureza*
(Variant of Sonns. 17, 131, and 153).

With such perfections Nature gave her care
  To form, gent Dame ! your figure's fair design,
  Yours bin a Beauty in this world divine,
Divine in graceful geste and airiest air :
Of sort your Beauty shows beyond Compare,
  In you so many graces purely shine,
  No Dame so 'sured that she deem her digne
To feel, you present, she can call her fair :

Toiled human Nature, till she could no more,
  To frame a model of such charm and grace,
When deckt with graceful charms your shape she bore :
  And, more to glorify that form and face,
After she framèd you at once she swore
  Ne'er more to forge for Soul so fair a Case.

## CCCVIII.

*D'amores de huma inclita donzella*
(Variant of Sonn. 137).

Smitten with love of inclyt Damosel
   The God of Love his very self did see,
   Confined, in fine, the more he'd fain go free
From charms all conquer, all to yield compel :
Never saw mortal world such Bonnibel,
   When Nature gathered in this perfect She
   Graces that garrèd Love such wound to dree,
Laces ne force ne fraud shall countervail :

O seld-seen loveliness, O lovely lure !   ·
   Loveliness potent e'en to subjugate
     The very Love-god in his sovran reign :
     Look if a Human of so feeble strain
   Can, with his little force, bear force so great
When Love's own force so little could endure !

## CCCIX.

*Em hum batel que com doce meneio*
(Petrarch, I. 170).

In a slight Barque that softly, gently swaying
   Parted gold-rolling Tagus' wavy flow,
   I saw fair Ladies, liefer say I so
Fair Stars around one Central Sun a-raying
The Maids Nereian delicately playing
   Wi' thousand lays and liltings sweet and low
   In sport the beautiful array would row
(An err I not) for better honour paying.

O lovely Nereids! who with songs a-lift
  Haste that serenest vision to enjoy,
    Which on my life-tide wills such Ill to wreak ;
Tell her how passeth (look she !) passing swift
  Fleet-footed Time ; how tedious mine annoy,
    For Time be ready-strong and Flesh be weak.


## CCCX.

*Que fiz, Amor, que tu taõ mal me tratas,*
(By the Duque de Aveyro ?).


What did I, Love, thou shouldst me so maltreat ?
  I not being thine why shouldest will me ill ?
  And why, if holden thine, thus spoil and spill
My wretched Life-tide made one long defeat ?
If bound to abet that cruel Nymph's deceit,
  And thou must haste her esperance full to fill,
  To whom shall I bewail what Ills thou will,
What life shalt give me after taking it ?


And thou (Unpitiful !) to my gloire and fame
  Mortal oblivion dost for boon return,
Aye disregarding so unguarded flame !
But since thou come not to thy lover's claim,
  Uncoming never shalt thou tidings learn
Of him who ever calleth on thy name.

## CCCXI.

*Se ao que te quero desses tanta fé,*
(Probably by Camoens, for a friend).

If in " I love thee " thou as much confide
  As be thou prodigal of heart-felt pain,
  My sighs of sorrow were not sighed in vain,
Nor had I vainly for thy favour cried.
But since thy harshness all belief denied
  To woes conditioned by thy coy disdain,
  With thee Unreason hath more might and main
Than all the tender love in me descried.

And since thou ever broughtst me Death so near
  With that Unlove which ne'er be mine behovèd, .
Yes, I will die, but know thy gain be dear !
  Asked o' thee daily mortal hearts commovèd
" Ah why hast murthered, Ladye cruel-fere !
  The one who loved thee more than life he lovèd?"

## CCCXII.

*O Tempo está vingado à custa mia*
(Connected with Nos. 5 and 150).

Time is avengèd (costing me so dear)
  On time, when Time I wont so cheap to rate ;
  Sad whoso was of Time in like estate
That Time at every time spent free o' fear !
Chastised me Time and Obstinacy sheer
  Because wi' Time I did miscalculate,
  For Time hath so untimely left my fate
Now hope I nothing from good timely chear.

Times, hours and moments swiftly, surely past,
    When I could profit of my Time and tide,
With hope that Time my tormentrye outlast :
    But when in Time I ventured to confide,
As Time hath various motion, slow and fast,
    I chid myself that Time I mote not chide.

## CCCXIII.

*Quem busca no amor contentamento,*
(Sufistical).

Whoso Contentment seeks in Love to find,
    Finds what his Nature deemeth suitable ;
    But Substance, balancing twixt Good and Ill,
Is but a leaflet whirling in the wind.
Who to such Mobilè hath self resignèd
    E'en his own glory holds not at his Will :
    In constant quality ne'er 'tis equable,
Since for his torment 'tis of fleeting kind.

Thus find we Love displaying, day by day,
    In single Subject two contending Foes,
        Which be, peraunter, thus of Fate ordainèd :
Now one way straying then on other way,
    Or to the lover's lucre or his loss,
        But ne'er one moment to despair constrainèd.

## CCCXIV.

*Se a ninguem tratais com desamor,*
(Cf. Ode IV. 3 and 4).

An with Unlove you deign no man to treat,
 Nay, love you general loving to repart,
 Showing to each and every self-same heart
Plenisht wi' gentle chear, wi' love replete :
Me fro' this day entreat with hate and heat,
 Display me coy disdain, do cruel smart ;
 Then shall I haply hold in whole and part
Me only holdest for thy favours meet.

For an thou deal sweet doles to every wight,
 'Tis clear thy favour won he, he alone
To whom thou showest anger and despight.
 Ill could I weet my love thy love has won
If wone another love within thy sprite :
 Love owns no partnership : No ! Love is one.

## CCCXV.

*Gostos falsos de amor, gostos fingidos,*
(Written in absence, probably in India).

False Gusts of Love, feigned Gusts for ever feigning,
 Vain Gusts by narrow limits limited,
 Great Gusts the while in Fancy born and bred,
Small Gusts when all the gain was lost by gaining ;
Wasted ere won, forlore before the attaining,
 E'en at the first beginning finishèd ;
 Changeful, inconstant, hotly hurrièd,
Appearing, disappearing, waxing, waning :

I lost you losing all my hope to see
 Aught of recovery; now I hope no higher
Than with your Sovenance see you cease to be
 For if my Life-tide and my Fancy tire
O' Life so far fro' you, more tireth me
 Remembering days when mine was my Desire.


## CCCXVI.

*Com o tempo o prado seco reverdece,*
(By the mystic, Balthazar Estaço?).

Wi' Time the wilted meadow waxeth green,
 Wi' Time in glooming grove the leaflet lies,
 Wi' time the mighty stream more gently hies,
Wi' Time grow fat and rich fields poor and lean :
Wi' Time this day is stormy, that serene,
 Wi' Time this bay-wreath blooms, that laurel dies
 Wi' Time hard painful Evil fleets and flies,
Wi' Time our vanisht Weals again are seen :

Wi' Time shall niggard Fate a change bestow,
 Wi' Time high station falls annihilate,
 Wi' Time returns it higher still to soar.
Wi' Time shall all things come, shall all things go,
 Only the passèd Time who ganged his gait
 Wi' Time a present Time becomes no more.

## CCCXVII.

*Aquelles claros olhos que chorando*
(Written in India ?).

Those brightly beaming Eyne with tearful stain
    Bedimmed I saw the while fro' them I hied,
    What do they now?  Who shall to me confide
An for an absent aught to care they deign ?
If they in memory hend or how or when
    I saw from joyaunce self so wide and side ?
    Or if they figure the glad time and tide
(That happiest day) when I their sight regain ?

If count they hours and how each moment flees ?
    If in one instant many years they live ?
If they confabulate with bird and breeze ?
O happy Visions ! blessèd Phantasies
    That in this absence thoughts so sweet can give
And know to gladden saddest reveries !

## CCCXVIII.

*Ausente dessa vista pura e bella*
(Written in India?).

While from that pure belle Vision driven afar
    Which erst made life-tide ever glad and gay,
    Now on my absent Life such agonies prey
As did your presence every bane debar :
Cruel and direful call I that dure Star
    Which drives my joys fro' you so far away,
    Banning a thousand times the hour, the day,
The curst beginning of such angry jar :

And I so tortured in this absence wone,
  Doomèd by destined, ever-cruel Power
  A dule so singular in this world to dree.
Long had I patience far fro' me out-thrown
  Nor less my Life, by force of this same stowre,
  Did I not cherish life your sight to see.


## CCCXIX.

*Saudades me atormentão taõ cruelmente,*
(Written in India ?).

Repining pains me with so fierce intent,
  Repine for pleasure past and weal bewray'd ;
  So much of Evil ne'er my doom was made
Sans reason, sithence I can self absent :
For Love I saw me whilom all-content,
  For Love I willèd life by pain waylaid ;
  'Tis right I see mine error so well paid
As now, when present griefs and pains torment.

For well deserved I, faring far fro' you,
  To unsee you, Ladye ! nor you see me more,
That with my life-tide I defray my due :
  But, as my Spirit doth its sin deplore,
Bid me not weep lost lot, and grant I view
  With gladdened eyes one softening glance some hour.

## CCCXX.

*O dia, hora ou o ultimo momento*
(Written in India?).

The day, the hour, the moment of that hour
   Which ends a life-tide Destiny so mismade,
   I view already Esperance waylaid,
Nor Thought shall trick me with her snaring power.
Shifts full of tristesse, Severance full of stowre,
   Faring that saw me forfeit, soon as said,
   What my long service merited be paid ;
O ! how by changing Change can all deflower !

No more I hope to sight the things gone by,
   I see that Parting, now prolonged so long,
Hopes of returning to my heart deny :
   My little tale is tattled by the throng,
Right well I weet 'twas mine to verify
   Such long-drawn Partings to short life belong.

## CCCXXI.

*Se para mim tivera, que algum dia*
(Written in India? Cf. Canz. XI.).

Could I for self expect that some one day,
   Moved by the Passion which my torments vent
   You mote a something sense of sentiment
For one who seeth rest none other way ;
Mine Ills for Glories I to heart would lay,
   And hold as pleasures whatso pains have shent ;
   And, in the midst of Discontent, content
Sweet Memory's orders I would fain obey.

Woe worth the day ! What thoughts my sprite be firing
  O' things that hasten faster to entomb me,
    For pay of summer-madness so notorious !
What serves my purpose this so fond desiring,
  When your deserving and my Destiny doom me
    To doubt such glory that can dub me glorious?


## CCCXXII.

*Oh fortuna cruel ! oh dura sorte !*
(Imitation of Camoens ?).


Ay, cruel Fortune ! Ay, dure lot of woe !
  Labour that placed me in so parlous state,
    No disillusion now will I await,
For Death's the only cure my care shall know :
" Art blind ? " (quoth Love) " so stark thyself to show
  'Gainst one who fareth ever aggravate
    While doing thee service, and disconsolate
With heart sore harmèd by thy swashing blow? "


But now as Destiny wills me worst of will
  Ay cruel Fortune mine ! O Amor, grant
As least of guerdon leave to wail my fill :
  For in such travail, woe so puïssant,
Ill could I (lacking it) console mine Ill,
  Now that none other boon of thee I want.

## CCCXXIII.

*Perder-me assi em vosso esquecimento*
(Metaphysico-amorous, by Camoens?).

Thus from your Thought to lose me nills consent
　My very Being by your charms o'erthrown ;
　Yet I, so being a being to you beknown,
Or e'en consented, now shall rest content.
But when you careless deign such Coyness vent
　On one who merits every kindness shown,
　Tho' ne'er my spirit shall the offence condone,
Far more offendeth me your meritment.

That you bear blame endureth not my Will,
　You to myself I 'trusted, Ladye mine !
　　Sans aught of unbecoming blot or tache.
Then show your Countenance pity for mine Ill,
　As Love there wones with every Grace, in fine,
　　And all perfection doth to you attach.

## CCCXXIV.

*Se alguma hora em vós a piedade*
(Written when going to India ?).

If haply rue you, in some happy hour,
　Your deme of torments that so long tormented,
　Love shall denay Consent that fare contented
Far from your dearest eyes my pine-full stowre.
Fro' you I fare me, but the Will whose power
　Your form fro' Nature on my soul depainted,
　Bids me believe this absence feigned and fainted,
But how much worse when I its truth discoure !

I must go, Ladye! and fro' you begone,
  My tristful tears shall take revenge in kind
On eyne whose daily bread were you alone.
Life I'll surrender by its pains undone,
  For here my Memory me, in fine, shall find
Ensepulchrèd in your Oblivion.


## CCCXXV.

*Já tempo foi que meus olhos traziam*
(Not by Camoens?).


Time was mine Eyes delighted to unfold
  Some gladsome tidings to my mind's Intent;
  Time was when every sense and sentiment
Rejoiced to savour what to me they told:
Love and Love-longings throngèd then to hold
  A general meeting in my breast content,
  While on her firm foundations Esperance leant
And glosing quiddities turned out a-cold.

That Nymph of mine then waxing less humane
  Smote Love with careless glance, a two-edged Sword,
O saddest Ill! O cruel Feliciane!
  Complaints with Jealousy, meseems, accord,
Yet—no for certain! nor is such my bane:
  My Faith in justice speaks this bitter word!

------

## CCCXXVI.

*Quão bem aventurado me achára,*
(Imitation of Camoens?).

With what high blessing me had Fortune blest
    Would Love such favour on my lot bestow,
    And thus, while least of boons he willèd show,
With show of greater would content my breast.
Entire and parfit Weal had I possest,
    Did not my longings long more Weal to know;
    But now (when seen you) I deserve to owe,
At least, the object of my longing quest.

Yet these Desires with this exceeding Dare
    Were born of me when 'twas my Sort to sight you,
        And wax they stronger, Dame! with every sight.
Desire fro' Fancy's hand I strave to tear,
    For 'tis my firm belief 'twill only flyte you,
        But thrives it evermore the more I fight.

## CCCXXVII.

*Si el triste coraçon que siempre llora,*
(Spanish: written during first exile?).

If the triste heart that Weeping e'er must dree,
    Yet lacks what maketh Weeping meritorious,
    Could 'joy already joys of fight victorious,
Won in Love's warfare worse'd by victory;
If, now enshadowèd by the greeny tree,
    I feed of Phantasies the flock memorious
    Well mote I 'joy Joy's height I hold most glorious
Could I one moment my Pastora see:

Then, neither Air, with airy sighs besigh'd
   For Love, could deal my Dolours increment
Nor fount-full eyelids feed this founty tide.
   But, to despoil me of all jolliment,
A passion bids from her I absent 'bide
Who ne'er is absent fro' my Soul and Sent.

## CCCXXVIII.

*Do estan los claros ojos que colgada*
(Spanish : written in exile ?).

Where be those clearest orbs that wont to bear
   In suite and following my surprizèd sprite?
   Where be those cheeks with rosy splendour dight
Surpassing roses of the rarest rare ?
Where be the red red lips so debonnair
   Adorned with teeth no snow was e'er so white?
   The tresses starkening golden metal's light
Where be they? and that dainty hand, ah where ?

O lovely all ! where hidst thou evermore
   That I may never see thee, whom to see
My great Desire destroys me every hour !
   But look no longer on this vainest plea,
Still in my spirit I my Ladye store,
   And ask where hidest thou fro' sight of me !

## CCCXXIX.

*Ventana venturosa, do amanece*
(Spanish : for a friend ?).

Thou winsome Window! whence the Morns dispread
    My Ladye's splendour with Apollo's glow,
    Mote I behold thee firèd with such lowe
As that such splendour in my spirit bred !
For an thou see what Ills I sufferèd
    And feel the dule aye firing soul so woe,
    Why to my longing eyes the Couch ne'er show,
The flower-bed flourishing with tears I shed ?

If nothing move thee now my painful plight,
    Leastwise commove thee sight óf that small gain
Gainèd when joyaunce thou deniest my sprite.
    Now since thou connst it, Casement unhumàne !
E'er Day my dule discoure to mortal sight,
Grant I behold my Nymph, my suzerain.

## CCCXXX.

*De piedra, de metal, de cousa dura,*
(Spanish : a conceit).

With stone, with metal, substance cold and dure,
    My Nymph enclothes her soul, the dure, the cold,
    The locks be woven of the cold dure gold,
The brow is whitest marble's portraiture :
The eyne are dyed with smaragd's verd' obscure,
    The cheeks granadoes, and the feigning mould
    Of lips is ruby none may have in hold ;
The snow-white teeth show pearly lustre pure :

The hand be youngest ivory and the throat
　Of alabaster ivy-clipt, whereon
　　The veins are skeins of lazuli rutilant :
But what in all of you most awèd I note,
　Is seeing, albe all of you be stone,
　　You bear embosomed heart of diamant.


## CCCXXXI.

*Al pie de una verde e alta enzina*
(Spanish : a little Idyll).


At foot of lofty holm, in verdant shade,
　Awakèd Corydon his viol's sound,
　　O'erhung by felting ivy, spireing round
The bole, and flaunting to the branching head.
He sang the love he bore that lovely maid,
　May Amaryllis, who his bonds had bound ;
　　The birds go coursing o'er the boughen-ground,
A chrystal fountain playeth through the glade :

To him draws Tityrus near in reverie lost,
　Driving his weary flock wi' hunger spent :
This was the Shepherd-friend he lovèd most,
　Who sang the sorrows which his heart had rent :—
Nor alien speech for grieving Soul hath gust,
　Nor grief of alien grieveth Heart content.

## CCCXXXII.

*Amor, Amor, que fieres al coitado*
(Spanish : copy corrupt).

Love ! Love ! who joyest aye the wretch to smite
   Which for thy love did service many a year,
   Thy service bearing, maugre snares so fere ;
In fine, fine never looked-for hast thou dight.
With lonesome Dolours, with a care-full Sprite
   Ensnared, thou payest service bought so dear,
   Cases so strange, unheard by human ear,
For thee enduring like no mortal wight.

Who deems thee godhead he's gone mad I vouch,
   Who holds thy justice fails in equity,
For least he gains who serves thee long and much.
   Let thy believers deem the worst of me,
I judge from whatso see I and I touch
   And hardly trust I what I touch and see.

## CCCXXXIII.

*Fermoso Tejo meu quam differente*
(Attributed to three other writers).

My lovely Tagus ! with what different Sent
   I saw and see thee, me thou sawst and se'est :
   I see thee turbid, me thou seest triste,
I saw thee limpid, me thou sawst content :
Changed thee a Freshet, flooding vehement,
   Which thy large valley faileth to resist :
   Changed me her Favour dealing, as she list,
Or life contented or life miscontent.

Now that in evils be we partners twain,
    So be 't in welfare; ah! mote I but see
We two were likest in our bliss and bane!
    When a new Prime shall bloom with brightest blee
What erst thy being was shalt show again:
    I n'ote if what I was again shall be.


## CCCXXXIV.

*Memorias offendidas que hum só dia*
(On the death of a lover).


Offended Memories! that no single day
    Unto my brooding Thoughts a rest have lent,
    My taste of torments may ye ne'er prevent,
Whom you offend he fended you alwày.
If well ye will me, look how ye bewray
    The dainty blossoms of that sentiment
    She left, when I to eternal Exile went
From her fere Death undid to cold dead clay.

She left me pining for my past offence;
    She stole my single, sole-remaining cure
        Which could warray all woes that worse my sprite.
Where shall my losses look for recompense,
    When on my sorrow doth my Luck assure
        It ne'er shall lend my life one moment's light?

## CCCXXXV.

*Lembranças tristes, para que gastais tento*
(On the death of a lover).

Ye tristeful Souvenirs ! why this vain intent
  Of over-tiring heart so tired by Fate ?
  Rest ye contented seeing me in such state,
Nor fro' me seek ye greater meritment.
I fear you little whatso pangs ye vent,
  Wont in my wonted woes to gang my gait ;
  I feel mine Evils weigh so weighty weight,
No Weal my hapless me can now content.

In vain I labour when to harm I sought
  One who has lost his hopes in long-drawn strife,
  One dead to all he once desirèd see :
From overlosing I to lose have naught,
  Sauf this already worn and weary life
  Which, for my sorer loss, survives in me.

## CCCXXXVI.

*Quando descançareis, olhos cansados !*
(Probably written in India).

When shall ye rest you, Eyne that look for rest !
  Since Her who lent you life no more you view ;
  Or when shall view you wishing long adieu
To your misfortune's immemorial quest ?
Or when shall hard-heart Fate vouchsafe behest
  My ruined Esperance in my soul renew,
  Or when (if every Hope be lost to you)
With by-gone blessings can ye make me blest ?

This pine shall do me die right well I ween,
    Wherein my hoping were like whistle o' wind ;
      Then nowise hope I my desire be dight :
And when so truly the sore truth I've seen,
    Come every possible pain for me design'd
      As naught affrights me what each day I sight.


## CCCXXXVII.

*Memoria de meu bem cortado em flores,*
(Probably written in India).


Memories of Joyaunce ! nipt in budding flow'r
    By the frore fingers of my fere Misfate,
    Vouchsafe a gracious rest my cares abate
In my Love's ever restless, ceaseless stowre.
Suffice me Ills and Fears that present low'r
    For ever threating Chance unfortunate,
    Without return of long-past happy state
To affront with dolours every happy hour.

I lost in single hour what I in time
    So large, so slowly minuting, had gain'd :
      Dreams of this glory fly ye, far go flee.
My life needs perish in this desert-clime
    For here I 'm fated with mine Ills to end
      Not one but thousand lives, hard Memory !

## CCCXXXVIII.

*Do corpo estava já quasi forçada,*
(Variant of the immortal No. 19).

Enforced by greater force well-nigh had fled
  Its frame that gentle Soul to Heaven due,
  Rending her noble webs of Life she flew
For faster 'turning to her patrial stead.
Still flowering, blooming, ere her root had spread
  In Earth she hated with a hate so true,
  Self she uprooted and departing drew
Fro' Death a sweetness for that journey dread.

Pure Soul, who self to mortal world hast shown
  Free from its fetters which the lave enlace,
    For few short hours exchanging fair long years :
Of thine, thou leftest 'lone in woe to wone,
  Move thee high Pity, while so slowly pace
    These hours made slower by our tristful tears.

## CCCXXXIX.

*O dia, hora em que naci moura e pereça,*
(A Threnody : certainly by Camoens).

Die an eternal Death my natal Day,
  May Time that hapless date unknow, unlearn ;
  May 't ne'er return and, if it need return,
Blackest eclipse the bright Sun overlay !
Fail of his splendour Sol's resplendent ray,
  Earth ! show relapse to chaos' reign forlorn,
  Air ! rain thou blood ; all monster-births be born
And may the Mother cast her bairn away !

Then shall the peoples in amazed distress,
  With cheeks tear-stainèd, bosoms horror-fraught,
    Expect a shattered world eftsoons to sight.
Fon race ! on similar fancies lay no stress ;
  For on this Day to light a life was brought
    The most unhappiest life e'er brought to light.


## CCCXL.

*Transumpto sou, Senhora, neste engano,*
(To a Lady fain of gifties).


I am translated, Ladye ! by your snare,
  And snaring-practise mote to me be sparèd ;
    Hardly can mortal man by you be snarèd
Who could from other yous unsnarèd fare.
Now well I weet me, 'twas at cost of care
  When you for nothing save sweet gifties carèd,
    But, as your judgment hath of me declarèd,
This year's expectancy goes vain and bare.

Of Love I treated long, but now my sight
  Easily seeth Feignery and its aim ;
    For so doth seem, gent Dame ! whate'er you show.
Your very cunning holp you to this sleight,
  Claim fro' me only what I care you claim
    Or else 'tis uphill way you please to go.

## CCCXLI.

*Ondas que por el mundo caminando*
(Spanish : written in Africa ?).

Waves that encircle all the globe, with flow
　Onborne for ever by the legier breeze,
　　Bear, in your bosoms borne, my reveries
Where bides who, whereso biding, bodes she Woe
Tell her I only heap on woes a throe,
　Tell her my life may not one moment please ;
　　Tell her Death nills to slay my tormentries,
Tell her I live yet every Hope forgo.

Tell her how lost when found anew you me,
　Tell her how in my gain you lost my Sprite,
Tell her how lifeless cruelly slew you me.
　Tell her how came you me the Smit to smite,
Tell her how undone did undo you me,
　Tell her how saw me only hers your sight.

## CCCXLII.

*Sobre un olmo que al cielo parecia*
(Spanish).

Percht on sky-climbing Elm, that showèd nude
　Of bloom and leafage, saw I saddest show—
　　A lone and widowed Bird who whelmed in woe
More solitary made the solitude :
O'er a clear Fount that sea-ward path pursue'd
　With mournful dulcet murmur bent she low,
　　And with her plungèd plume disturbed its flow
And drank the water seen it muddy-hue'd.

The cause that cast her down in grievous care
  Was the lone Turtle's sense of severance :
Behold how Severance mortal griefs can bear !
  An love and parting have such vehemence,
And to unreasoning Bird so deal despair,
  Say what shall sense he that hath sent and sense ?

## CCCXLIII.

*Cançada e rouca boz por que bolando*
(Spanish : written by Camoens ?).

Weary harsh-sounding Voice ! why take not flight
  And where lies sleeping my Florinda wend ;
  And there of all things whereto I pretend
Why not, O happy Voice ! enjoy delight?
Go soft, and sighing in her ear alight,
  And unheard tell her, though she ne'er attend,
  I dree such Evils only Death can end
And I am singing when to die I'm dight.

And tell her, though her counterfeit I hold
  Here to my 'biding I would see her hieing,
Would she not find her lover lifeless-cold.
  But ay ! I n'ote what say you save I'm dying,
Because so near her beauties to behold
  Yet ne'er beholding what I die for 'spying.

## CCCXLIV.

*O capitão Romano esclarecido,*
(Alluding to Albuquerque and Ruy Dias?).

The Roman Capitayne so famed of yore,
   Sertorius, second never found in fight,
   Such lofty model to us mortals dight
That ne'er was heard of, ne'er was seen before.
Sith for a soldier who his oath forswore,
   Doing a villein deed of base-born wight,
   He dealt so terrible and so dread requite,
Wherefore his Many feared him ever more.

What made the Chief that Legion decimate?
   For-that it failèd do the duties owe'd
     To grim and grisly, hard and horrid Mart.
O clear example! Captain forceful great,
   Who upon Roman men the lore bestow'd
     Of soldier Science, of invincible Art!

## CCCXLV.

*A Roma populaça proguntava*
(Apology for marriage : by Camoens?).

Happed of the Roman populace to speer
   A certain curious Wit, a careless Wight,
   Wherefore in general do the kye delight
To pair at certain seasons of the year?
Whereto as Folk discreet, which would appear
   Responsive soaring to an eminent height,
   They by a single phrase threw notable light
On the dark theme and showed what held they dear.

This was the intention :—" Brutes may not intend
  How fair fruition and what weighty worth
    Have Hymen's fetters binding man's desire :
But brutaller Bestials they who e'er pretend
  In flesh a pleasure find, find joy on Earth,
    Leaving their Souls to feed the Eternal Fire.


## CCCXLVI.

*Com o generoso rostro alanceado*
(One of the last written by Camoens).


With sign of lance-thrust on his generous face,
  And smircht his Royal brow with dust and blood,
    To Charon's gloomy bark on Acheron flood
Came great Sebastiam—shade in shadowy place.
The cruel Ferryman, seen the forceful case,
  Whenas the King would pass opposing strode,
    And cried "None tombless o'er this flood e'er yode
For all Unburieds on the shore must pace."


Commoved the valorous King with kindled ire
  Replies : " False Greybeard ! haply wouldst assure
    None past yon side by force of golden ore ?
    Durst thou with Monarch bathed in Moorman gore
  Chaffer of funeral pomps, of sepulture ?
From one less wealthy o' wound thy fee require ! "

## CCCXLVII.

*Quando do raro esforço que mostravas*
(On the brave death of a young soldier).

When thy rare Valiancy in battle shown
   To gather warfare's largest fruit ne'er failèd,
   Fate shore thy flowering age, whose feats prevailèd
O'er the short year-tale thou couldst call thine own.
Set in its helmet-frame thy face outshone
   When visor-veilèd Mars, Amor unveilèd :
   If oped thy Sabre serried squads assailèd
Thy geste of Beauty Beauty's eye-glance won.

No steel of foeman, no ! could doom thee bleed ;
   'Twas Vulcan's deed, the god whose forceful might
   Enpierceth surest harness part and part :
But he, for pardon of his fault shall plead,
   He deemèd, seeing thy bravery beauty-dight,
   Thou wert a son of Venus sire'd by Mart.

## CCCXLVIII.

*Quam cedo te roubou a morte dura*
(Of D. Alvaro da Silveira slain and unburied ?).

How soon hath stole thy life Death sore and dure
   Illustrious Spirit wont to soar and stye ?
   Leaving thine outcast, clay-cold corse to lie
In strangest albe noble sepulture !
Fro' Life, whose duraunce here may not endure,
   Already bathèd in the Foe's red dye,
   Raised by thy Valour's forceful hand on high
Thou winnest Immortal Fields where Life is sure.

The Spirit joyeth happy time eterne ;
The Corse, that earthly grave could not contain,
    Earth bade her feathered children bear their prey.
Thou leftest every heart to pine and yearn ;
    Thou soughtest honourèd death on Honour-plain :
    Our Tagus bare thee, Ganges bore away.


## CCCXLIX.

*A ti, Senhor, a quem as Sacras Musas*
(To his uncle D. Bento de Camoens ?).


To thee, Senhor ! whose Soul the sacred Muses
    Feed with a portion of their food divine,
    Not they of Delian fount nor Caballine,
Which be Medeas, Circès and Medùses ;
But the gent bosoms wherein Grace infuses
    Arts which to heavenly laws o' grace incline,
    Kindly of doctrine and wi' Love benign,
Not they whom blinded Vanity confuses ;

This feeble offspring, and the latest bearing
    Of mine intelligence in weakly way,
        To thee a warm affection proffereth.
But an thou notice it as over-daring,
    Here for that daring I would pardon pray,—
        Pardon my Heart's affection meriteth.

———

## CCCL.

*Tu, que descanso buscas com cuidado,*
(On the Redemption).

Thou who with restless Hope to rest thee tried
    Upon this mundane Life's tempestuous Main,
    Hope not fro' travail any rest attain,
Save rest in CHRIST, the JESU crucified.
If toil for riches bring thee sleepless tide,
    In Him is found immeasurable gain ;
    If of true formosure thy Soul be fain,
This Lord espying in His love shalt 'bide :

If worldly pleasure or delight thou seek,
The sweets of every sweet He holds in hoard,
Delighting all with joys o'er Earth victorious.
If haply gloire or honours thou bespeak,
What can more honour bring, what bin more glorious
Than serve of highest lords the highest Lord ?

## CCCLI.

*O gloriosa Cruz, O victorioso*
(Of Dom Sebastiam's Banner?   Cf. Sonn. 243).

O glorious Cross ! O Cross for aye victorious !
    Trophy that every mortal spoil containeth ;
    O chosen signal which to worlds ordaineth
A Panacea marvellous and memorious !
O Living Fount that Holy Water raineth !
    In Thee our every bane its balm obtaineth,
    In Thee the Lord, " Almighty " titled, deigneth
Assume of Merciful the Name most glorious.

In Thee was ended dreadful Vengeance-day,
In Thee may Pity bear so fairest flower
As Prime that followeth Winter's injury.
Vanish all foemen flying from Thy power ;
Thou couldst so potent change in Him display
Who never ceasèd what He was to be.

## CCCLII.

*Mil vezes se move meu pensamento*
(Imperfect : Here Jur. ends).

For times a thousand mine Intent was bent
  To praise that forehead huèd chrystalline,
  Those ribbèd tresses shining golden Shine,
The clear mind passing man's intendiment ;
Which, wi' the softest, suavest movement, rent
  (Such was its might) the breast-plate diamantine ;
  Those sovereign Graces and that Air divine,
That honest pride with sweetest accent blent :

*The Roses lying in a waste of snow*
Those pearls of Morning-land, a chosen row,
Bedded in rubies smiling douce and gay :
The light those glorious Eyne on us bestow,
Shown by your gladdening smilet ever gay,
Is light from Heaven, a paradisial ray.

———

## CCCLIII.

*Queimado sejas tu e teus enganos*
(Braga, No. 300; Storck, 348).

Burn thou and burn wi' thee thy snaring Bane
  Love ! cruel fellow felonous and fell,
  Burnt be thine arrows, burn thy string as well
And Bow, the weapon working so much pain :
Thy covenanted promises prophane,
  Thy wheedlings honieder than Hydromel,
  All, all may see I, when wi' gall they swell,
Brent by the blaze wherewith thou burnest men.

I leave thee now, those eyën-strings untying,
  To sight the orbs wherewith my sprite hast tied,
  For well sufficeth thee such vengcänce.
But like the Wight of desperate wound a-dying,
  Ill shalt thou die if well the hurt thou hide
  Losing the single medicine—Esperance.

## CCCLIV.

*Senhora, quem a tanto se atreve*
(Braga, No. 304 ; Storck, 349).

Dame, whoso dareth hie to such a height
  He serve you, cherish you in Sovenance,
  Knowing such memory be sans esperance,
The dues he claimeth bin ne little ne light.
This Sprite holds more than what these Hands indite,
  Yet never hoping happy change of chance,
  Nor wishing other fair deliverance
Fairer than Love-debt to your service dight.

To hope for mighty chance from Aventùre
Would to your meritment but work offence,
And thus you pay the pains I underwent.
I hold impossible my Care to cure,
And still remain my sense and sentiment
In bond of debtor to your Formosure.


## CCCLV.

### *Angelica la bella despreciando*
(Spanish : Ariosto, XVIII. 165 ; Braga, 308 ; Storck, 350).

Angelica, the bellabone, misdeeming
    Whatever joys Time placed upon her way,
    Flouted with jeering laugh all men, that May
Kingdoms and knightly value scant esteeming.
Only of self and beauteous self aye dreaming
    Hied upon Frankish-land her steps one day,
    Where saw she lonely under a tree-shade lay
A hapless infant with his life-blood streaming.

She who had spurnèd Love and Love's behest,
    She who to all so cruel showed, so dure,
Within her sensed the boon of softening breast.
    Thus seeing Medòro doth her hele secure
And hence Love turnèd ill to good the best :
    In fine Love-chances all bin Aventùre.

————

## CCCLVI.

*La letra que s'el nombre en que me fundo*
(Spanish : to Luisa : Braga, 309 ; Storck, 351).

The leading letter on my building-ground
  Cometh the chiefest in my weary way,
  Justly the same was L, so men should say
Its light on lowly Earth, is loveliest found.
Thus eke the V, that formeth second sound,
  Voweth to Death all eyne her Light survey ;
  Then showeth Y that yearneth to warray
And maketh dying hour most joyous Stound.

Next cometh sign of S that doth sustain
  The Sovran Being in whose form consist
    Virtue and grace and gifts as many and high,
In fine all finisheth A, alluding plain      :
  At end, at end, to me the wretch so triste
    Whom Amor doomèd for her love to die.

## CCCLVII.

*Luiza, son tan rubios tus cabellos*
(Spanish : Braga, 312 ; Storck, 352).

Louise ! thy tresses wear so ruddy hues
  Sol but to see them would his car detain ;
  And, while their splendour gars his shine to wane,
Would lose his radiance, not thy vision lose.
Blest who, by worth empower'd, their glory view,
  Blester the hand that could one tress obtain,
  But blestest he who doth his Soul maintain
Only on glorious lights these locks diffuse.

Louise ! when shine and shimmer so immense
   Of hair that lighteth all the Loves wi' lowe
(And Love of other love claims recompense) ;
   Tho' scant I merit thou such gift bestow
Still claims to see one tress my sighting sense
   To pay my weeping and to pay my woe.


## CCCLVIII.

*Se, senhora Lurina, algum começo*
(Another Icarus : Braga, 338 ; Storck, 354).


If any fain begin, my Dame Lurine !
   A song commensurate with your due of praise,
   He first would note your hard unfavouring ways
As highest honour to my pen 'twould mean.
For if in hope to praise I intervene
   And to your world inspirèd self would raise,
   The Thought inspireth me with such amaze
That makes me, certès, more your worth misween.

This soaring you-ward, whom such gifts exalt
   Of so high ardour, of so ardent flame,
   Melteth my pinions boldly fugitive ;
And if I fall in Ocean of default,
   I to my failure give fair name and fame
   But who your Value's claim shall dare to give ?

———

## CCCLIX.

*Tristezas ! Com passar tristes gemidos*
(Jur. MS. ; Storck, 355).

Tristesse ! wi' tristest moans and groans I wone
  Thro' day, thro' night to Phantasy appealing :
  In this black cavern èxtreme sorrow feeling
To see my life-tide suchwise overthrown :
Hidden like shadows fly my years, and flown
  Leave naught of fruitage that can work my healing,
  Save but to see them passing, whirling, wheeling
With Fortune's whirlgig till no sense I own.

In such imaginings, in tristest way
My Soul turns giddy, nor I sense in Sent
If I with any one say words I say ;
And, if of anything my Thoughts take tent,
I cannot say, while so my woes torment,
An fare I sane of sense or fare I fey.

## CCCLX.

*Dexadme, cantinelas dulces mias*
(Spanish : an Adieu : Storck, 356 and 439).

Leave me, ye douce melodious Lays o' mine,
  Leave me, ye rustick Pipes of sweet accord ;
  Leave me, clear Founts and leas of greeny sward,
Leave me, glad Garths all shadow and sunshine :
Leave me, ye Pastimes of my pride-full syne
  Leave me, ye Dances round the festal board ;
  Leave me the Pleasures flutes and flocks afford,
Leave me, ye Slumbers 'mid the sleepy kine.

Leave me, ye Stars and Moon and eke thou Sun,
   Leave me to mourn where tristest shades dismay me,
Leave me sans joy 'twixt Pole and Pole to run ;
   Leave me, sweet Prizes that to death betray me :
Yea ! leave me all in fine and leave me none
   Save Dule and Dolour which are dight to slay me !

www.ingramcontent.com/pod-product-compliance
Lightning Source LLC
Chambersburg PA
CBHW030349270326
41926CB00009B/1015